THE GUINNESS BOOK OF
ALMOST EVERYTHING YOU
DIDN'T NEED TO KNOW ABOUT

DOGS

Valerie Porter

GUINNESS BOOKS

EDITOR: Honor Head
DESIGN AND LAYOUT: Michael Morey

© Valerie Porter and Guinness Superlatives Ltd, 1986

Published in Great Britain by Guinness Superlatives Ltd,
33 London Road, Enfield, Middlesex

Typeset in 9/10 ITC Century Light
by Fakenham Photosetting Ltd, Fakenham, Norfolk
Printed and bound in Great Britain by R. J. Acford, Chichester, Sussex

'Guinness' is a registered trade mark of Guinness Superlatives Ltd

British Library Cataloguing in Publication Data

Porter, Valerie
    The Guinness book of almost everything you
    didn't need to know about dogs.–
    (Guinness oddfax)
    1. Dogs
    I. Title
    636.7   SF426

ISBN   0–85112–482–8

Valerie Porter has always shared her life with dogs and other animals. When she was a child the family home was full of dogs, cats, and all kinds of orphaned or injured wild animals and birds. She had a spell as a kennelmaid, working with champion standard poodles and lhasa apsos; she has kept her own various mongrels (and house cows and calves) and looked after numerous dogs for friends–boisterous Irish setters, clever lurchers, assorted labradors, alsatian crosses, collies and mongrels.

Dogs apart, she has written books on animals as different as cows and ferrets; about caring for pets and farm livestock, and about the countryside, wildlife, agriculture and old houses.

Contents

🐶 Cultured Dogs *87*

🏠 In a Word *115*

King Charles spaniels *by Edwin Landseer*

To be liked is very human. One of the reasons why we like dogs is that dogs are so ready to like us. A dog can find, even in the most worthless of us, something to believe in.

E. V. Lucas
The More I See Of Men

In the Beginning

Only two animals have entered the human household otherwise than as prisoners and become domesticated by other means than those of enforced servitude: the cat, and the dog.

Konrad Lorenz
Man Meets Dog

The dog has been domesticated for some fourteen or fifteen thousand years: it was man's first true companion among the many creatures with whom he shared this earth. All over the world, men have tamed members of the dog family—wolves, jackals and coyotes can still interbreed with domestic dogs and they share many characteristics of physiology and behaviour. Chance proximity led the North American Indians to tame the coyote, while the South American Indians domesticated the fox-like *Dusicyon* genus, halfway between the true vulpine foxes and the canid wolves. The ancestors of most of today's domesticated dogs are the wolf and the jackal.

The Dog Family

The dog is a member of the Canidae family, which includes:

Canis lupus–the **Wolf**, or Gray, White or Timber wolf

C. rufus–the **Red Wolf**

C. latrans–the **Coyote**, or Prairie or Brush wolf

C. dingo–the **Dingo**

C. familiaris–the **Domestic Dog**

C. aureus–the **Common Jackal**, or Golden jackal

C. mesomelas–the **Silver-Backed Jackal**

C. simensis–the **Simien Jackal**

C. adustus–the **Side-striped Jackal**

Vulpes–the **Vulpine Foxes**

Dusicyon–the **South American Foxes**

Alopex lagopus–the **Arctic Fox**, or Polar, White or Blue fox

Otocyon megalotis–the **Bat-eared Fox**

Lycaon pictus–the **African Wild Dog**, or Cape hunting dog, Tri-coloured dog or Wild dog

Cuon alpinus–the **Dhole**, or Asian wild dog or Red dog

Chrysocyon brachyurus–the **Maned Wolf**

Nyctereutes procyonoides–the **Raccoon Dog**

Speothos venaticus–the **Bush Dog**, or Vinegar fox

Wild Dogs

The **Dingo** (or Warrigal) is the only true wild dog and it is also probably the only purebred domesticated dog in the world (a skeleton believed to date from about 1,000 BC is identical in form to the modern dingo). The animal has interbred with the domestic dog and produced many local varieties of 'wild' and feral dogs, like:

New Guinea singing dog
Malaysian wild dog
Siamese wild dog
Filipino wild dog
Pariah dog
Sinhala hound
Thai dog
Canaan dog

'Pariah' has come to be a general term for half-wild dogs that are seen everywhere in some parts of the world, in the cities and in the countryside. Though often feral, and living as scavengers, they can usually be tamed and trained. In appearance they tend to fall into five types: basenji, collie, dingo, greyhound and kuvasz. The pariah dogs of India are very like the local wolves, and throughout the world other dogs also resemble wolves – like the European and Asian sheepdogs, the Eskimo dogs and the Black Wolfdog of Florida.

The First Dogs

The earliest known example of a domesticated dog is possibly the remains of a specimen found in Iran, thought to be more than 11,000 years old. The remains of a dog found at the Starr Carr Stone Age settlement in Yorkshire have been dated to about 7,500 BC.

Mesolithic
First pictorial representation of dogs–Magdalenian fresco, Spain.

Neolithic
Evidence of bones gnawed by dogs near human habitation, also of buried dogs.

c.4,200 BC
Foundation of Susa culture– Susian pottery shows Saluki-type dogs.

c.4,000 BC
Evidence of 'Peat Dogs' or 'Swiss Lake Dweller Dogs' – spitz type.
Two Pharaoh-type hounds on circular disk.
Pharaoh-type hound *Breath of Life of Senbi* in painted relief, tomb chapel of Senbi (Prince of Cusae, ruler of XIV Nome of Upper Egypt).
Persian manuscript mentions 'water dogs'.

c.3,600 BC
Painting of dog, Hierakanopolis.

c.3,000 BC
Contemporary tombs depict Afghan-type hound in Ancient Egypt.

c.1,300 BC
Three spotted dogs (sight-hounds with red dalmatian-type markings and feathered tails) in fresco of boar hunt, at Mycenaean palace, Tiryns.

7th century BC
Massive crouching dog with huge head and shoulders, tiny waist; terracotta, Kotyle.

Lucky charms from 7th century BC Nineveh, Assyria.

6th century BC

Afghan pictorial fabric *Departure of Warrior* (in British Museum)– greyhound type with feathered tail like Afghan hound.

Dogs under table on leads in terracotta scene of banquet in honour of Herakles, Krater.

Attic drinking-cup showing pair of dogs with herdsman and flock.

5th century BC

Man playing with his dog, marble funerary stele, Sardis.

3rd century BC

Mosaic of staghunt with hounds (signed Gnosis), Pella.

2nd century BC

Satyr huntsman teasing his dog with a dead rabbit, marble relief.

1st century BC

Shar-pei dogs, statuettes, Han Dynasty.

Wall painting of shepherd and dog, Villa Pamphil.

AD 1st century

Diana the huntress in bronze with her big-footed, thickset dog, Lyon.

Pompeii

Preserved contorted body of chained dog trying to escape eruption of Vesuvius.

Picture of dog on a floor mosaic with the warning *Cave Canem* 'beware of the dog'.

Memorial to a dog which had saved a child's life.

2nd century

Antinous as Silvanus with dog, marble sculpture, Lanuvium.

2nd–4th century

Mithras slaying the bull–several depictions with dog licking the bull's wound.

4th century

Mithraic genius with prick-eared dog, marble, Sidon.

Hunt scene with dogs chasing

Egyptian relief of early mastiff.

hare, engraved on shallow glass cup, Bonn.

Hunting scene: bringing home the wild boar, with collared bobtailed dog.

5th century

Pastoral scene from Virgil manuscript including collared spotted dog.

6th century

Shepherd with goats and dogs, silver dish, USSR.

Ancient Breeds

Assyria

Great Dane type for hunting lion, bull, wild ass.

Greyhound type for coursing hare and deer.

Egypt

Hounds (Pharaoh and Afghan type).

Types like dachshund and greyhound.

Creamy mastiff war dog.

Turnspit.

Greece

Wolfdogs (e.g. hounds, Persian molussus).

Beagle type of scenting hound.

Roman sculpture of early greyhounds.

Ferocious large guard dogs for livestock and home.

Rome

Three major categories: *Canes villatici* (house), *C. pastorales* (shepherd), *C. venatici* (pugnaces or mastiff type, and sagaces or greyhound type).
Boarhound (probably Tibetan molussus type).
Greyhound and Italian greyhound. Longhaired and other terriers.

Mythological Dogs

Actaeon's Hounds Actaeon the hunter accidentally glimpsed the goddess Diana bathing. She changed him into a stag and he was pursued and killed by his own 50 hounds.

Argos was the very old dog who recognised Odysseus when he came home in disguise after 20 years. The dog died of joy.

Cerberus was the monstrous 50-headed watchdog of Hades.

Gargittios and **Orthos** were

Geryon's monster dogs, killed by Hercules. Orthos was the brother of Cerberus.

Laelaps was destined to catch whatever he chased, but he was put in pursuit of a vixen destined never to be caught . . .

Maera was Icarius's faithful dog who committed suicide by jumping into a well to join his murdered master. Icarius became the constellation Bootes, his daughter Erigone became Virgo, and Maera became the star Procyon which rises in July just before the Dog Star.

Xanthippus's Dog was so faithful that it swam alongside its master's ship all the way to the Greek island of Salamis when the Athenians fled there for safety in 480 BC.

Classical Dogs

Arrian, *On Hunting, XVI Hares*, gives full details of using 'fast Celtic hounds of our day'.

Dio Chrysostom, *Discourses, VII (Euboicus)* '. . . took to hunting, sometimes using dogs changed from sheepdogs into a type of late trained, rather slow hunting dog'.

Homer, *Iliad* Nine swift-footed dogs following four golden herdsmen walking beside cattle – savage lion attacks – dogs to the rescue, barking furiously.

Horace, *Epodes II: Daydreams of a Moneylender* '. . . with his pack of hounds from here, from there, he forces the fierce boars towards the ready nets'.

Horace, *Satires II: The Tale of*

the Town Mouse and the Country Mouse '... when the lofty hall resounded with the baying of Molossian hounds'.

Xenophon, *Oeconomicus: On Farm Management* '... and puppies too learn to do tricks'.

Virgil, *Georgics III: Animal Husbandry in Africa and Scythia* 'The African swain '... and Amyclaean dog'.

Fronto, *Letters II: Sheep on Highway* describes meeting a large flock of sheep with four dogs and two shepherds taking up the whole road.

Ambrose, *Duties of the Clergy III* 'We do not allow our dogs to come to our table and leave them unfed ...'

Ovid, *Calendar IV: Prayers to the Country Gods* '... and healthy too the sagacious pack of watch dogs'.

Propertius, *Elegies II: Cynthia on the Farm* '... and learn to give commands to an eager pack of hounds'.

Xenophon, *On Hunting VI: On Hare Hunting* 'Having tied each of the hounds ...' with full details of how to set about hunting hares with hounds. Xenophon also gives details of slipping a Spartan hound for chasing wild boar.

Venerated Dogs

America The Karok and Navaho Indians regarded the dog's close cousin, the coyote, as a great hero and divine benefactor known as the Fire Stealer. In Oregon the coyote inspired creative exploits, and on the Gulf Coast of eastern California the coyote or prairie wolf was the creative hero and chief supernatural being. The Tinneh Indians had a miraculous dog as their chief divine being: he could assume the form of a handsome young man and he became the first material of most things when he was torn to pieces by giants.

Arabia The Arabians thought so highly of their dogs that they were the first to give them medical attention. The Saluki was said to be the sacred gift of Allah.

Arctic The Eskimo looked upon the native dog as the father of the human family. Greenlanders believed that because dogs existed before mankind they had a certain presentiment of the future; they also thought that eclipses were caused by the sun being pursued by his brother the moon, and in that frightening event the women would take their dogs by the ears on the assumption that, knowing the future, if the dogs did not cry out under such treatment then the world was not about to be destroyed. The Siberian Yakuts thought rather less of dogs: they believed that the human soul entered animals after death, and the weakest would end up in a dog.

Egypt Dogs were idolised in Ancient Egypt. Members of the family shaved themselves to mourn a dead dog in the time of Herodotus. The 'watchful and faithful' Dog Star, Sirius, heralded the vital annual overflow of the Nile and was worshipped for that reason. The ancient god Anubis was probably a jackal, not a dog, but was greatly venerated. Dogs in general were still esteemed for their sagacity in the time of Pythagoras, when the Egyptians

Anubis.

believed that at the death of a human being the soul entered various animals (an idea Pythagoras brought back to Greece where he founded a sect). Egyptian dogs were protected from being killed; they were never considered to be subordinate animals; and they were often temple guards.

Ethiopia A dog was elected as king. If it fawned, it found the government was good; if it growled, it was bad.

Greece Hecate was a Greek goddess who bestowed wealth and the blessings of daily life; the dog was her favourite animal and was sacrificed to her.

Kalangs of Java practised the Cult of the Red Dog. Each family kept one in the house—probably a wooden image—which was worshipped after the death of a member of the family and burnt after a thousand days.

Nepal Dogs were worshipped at a festival called Khicha Puja.

Nosarii of Western Asia were said to worship a dog.

Peritas was Alexander the Great's favourite dog. A city was named after him, and his statue was placed in the square.

Persia In the Mithraic religion, the dog was venerated as the companion of Mithras, God of Light. The dog is always shown springing towards the wound in the side of a sacred bull which Mithras has subdued and reluctantly sacrificed.

Rome In contrast with the Egyptian attitude, Sirius the Dog Star presaged bad weather for the Romans, and for the Greeks. It brought the hottest part of the year, the 'dog days' of pestilence and drought. The Romans sacrificed red dogs at the feast of Floralia in an attempt to pacify Sirius. At the annual festival of Diana at Nemi (Vesta) which was celebrated all over Italy on 13 August, the hottest time of the year, hunting dogs were crowned. At the height of Roman civilisation, dogs were restricted to the privileged classes and the Romans were the first to feed their dogs regularly, but as the civilisation crumbled dogs gradually became outcasts and scavengers. Rome had been very impressed by the enormous and powerful mastiffs of Britain and they were brought home to fight in the arenas against wild animals and gladiators. They were also used as prize war dogs.

Thlinkiti had a god called Khanukh, a wolf. (The wolf was also associated with Zeus and

Apollo, and with North American dancing and secret societies.)

Despised Dogs

Biblical Dogs Throughout the Old and New Testaments the dog is despised as an abhorrent, unclean animal. The only polite reference to a dog is in the Apocrypha (Old Testament appendix), in the Book of Tobit. Tobias's Dog accompanied him on a journey to Ecbatana as a companion and friend–a very alien concept to the Semitic mind, and the dog does not appear in Aramaic or Hebrew versions.

Hindu dogs were despised as unclean animals, animated by wicked and malign spirits condemned to do penance for crimes in a previous existence. If a Hindu came into contact with a dog, he must purify himself. The greatest insult they could give to a European or Christian was to call him a dog.

Olde Englishe Dogges

Dogs were at first classified according to their role rather than their appearance or breed. For example:

Lemor, Lyemer or Lymehound or Inductor (lyam = leash): used to trace wounded quarry or to scent out fresh quarry and flush it by barking.

Rache or Ratch Hound: scenting hound.

Brach or Brachettus: general hunting dog.

Alant: for baiting bear and wild boar.

Velterer Langehren, Kenetty or Kenet: a small beagle type which chased hares.

Leverer, Mauleverer or Leverarius: hare and rabbit chaser.

Bandog: usually a mastiff type, tied up as a watchdog.

Hot-trod or Hotrod: for the immediate pursuit of cattle rustlers.

Turnspit: small dog with short bandy legs which paddled a wheel that turned the roasting-spit.

Classifications

How The Types Were Divided

10th Century	14th Century
Bloodhounds	Greyhounds
Spaniels	Spotted dogs
Shepherd Dogs	Lap dogs
House curs	
Mastiffs	

1576: Dr Johannes Caius (A court physician who wrote a book outlining the following types of dog of his day.)
Eight hunting varieties: Harrier, Terrier, Bloodhound, Gazehound proper, Greyhound (very swift Gazehound), Leviner (lurcher type), Tumbler (tripped up the prey), Night Cur or Stealer.

Spaniels: Land, Water and Toy.

Sheepdog, Mastiff, Turnspit.

Mongrels for specific jobs, e.g. butcher's dogs, dancer.

Head Shapes

One of the early classifications was by the shape of the head:

1 More or less elongated head,

narrowing parietals (e.g. greyhound).

2 Moderately elongated head, diverging parietals (e.g. spaniel, setter, pointer, sheepdog).

3 Muzzle more or less shortened, cranium elevated (e.g. some terriers, most toy dogs).

1863 Classifications (Craig's Universal Dictionary)

Shepherd's Dog

Cur dog (worthless and degenerate)

Greenland Dog

Bulldog (*Canis molossus*)

Mastiff (frightener of thieves)

Bandog (large fierce chained Bond Dog)

Dalmatian or Coach Dog

Irish Greyhound

Gazehound (courage and speed)

Greyhound and Italian Greyhound

Lyemer (originally Bloodhound, later mongrel)

Lurcher (mongrel greyhound)

Tumbler (greyhound-like, similar to lurcher, which tumbles before attacking prey)

Terrier (dog which goes to earth)

Beagle (smallest hunting dog for hare)

Harrier (hare hound)

Foxhound

Old English Hound

Kibblehound (with short, crooked legs like Dachshund)

Bloodhound or Sleuth Dog

Spanish Pointer

English Setter

Newfoundland Dog

Rough Water Dog

Large Water Spaniel

Springer

Cocker

King Charles's Dog

Pryame Dog (not defined)

Lion Dog

Comforter (small spaniel)

Turnspit (as a breed rather than a function)

Pug (dwarf, rather like mastiff or bulldog)

1884 E. L. Harting Classification by Ears

Wolflike/greyhound/spaniel/hound/mastiff/terrier.

19th Century Stonehenge Classifications (J. H. Walsh in *British Rural Sports*)

1 Dogs that FIND game for man, leaving him to kill (pointer, setter, spaniel, water spaniel)

2 Dogs that KILL game when found for them (English greyhound)

3 Dogs that FIND AND KILL their game (bloodhound, foxhound, harrier, beagle, otterhound, fox terrier, truffle dog)

4 Dogs that RETRIEVE game wounded by man (retriever, deerhound)

5 USEFUL companions (mastiff, Newfoundland, St Bernard, bulldog, bull terrier, terriers, sheepdogs, pomeranian, spitz, dalmatian)

6 LADIES' TOY dogs (King Charles spaniel, Blenheim spaniel, Italian greyhound, pug, Maltese, toy terriers/poodles,

lion dog, Chinese and Japanese spaniels).

1902 Encyclopaedia Britannica Classifications

Wolfdogs Semi-domesticated dogs throughout Northern regions, wolflike with erect ears, long woolly hair, e.g. Eskimo dogs (a reclaimed wolf), North American Indian dogs (very like coyote), Black Wolfdog of Florida, sheepdogs of Europe and Asia resembling local wolves, Indian pariah dogs.

Greyhounds Hunt by sight– English and Italian greyhounds, Scotch deerhound, Irish wolfhound (declared extinct at the time), silky-haired Oriental variations, hairless dogs of Central Africa, China, Central and Southern America, whippet (local English greyhound × terrier), lurcher (greyhound × sheepdog, or deerhound × collie).

Spaniels Highly intelligent with large brain. Divided into several types:
Field: Clumber, Sussex, Norfolk, Cocker
Water: Irish breeds best known. Poodle probably from spaniel
Smaller pets: best known King Charles and Blenheim
Setters: trained to crouch (English, Irish, Gordon, Russian)
Retrievers: (water spaniel × Newfoundland)
Newfoundland: simply an enormous spaniel
St Bernard: closely related to spaniel

Hounds Large dogs, hunt by smell, massive structure, large drooping ears, usually smooth coats–bloodhound, staghound (now extinct), foxhound, harrier, otterhound, beagle, turnspit (now extinct), basset hound, dachshund, pointer, dalmatian (light pointer).

Mastiffs Mastiff, bulldog, German boarhound, Great Dane, bull terrier, pugdog.

Terriers Very intelligent and trainable. Many breeds, all highly artificial and many highly overbred.

Extinct Breeds

Talbot Hound–probably the original scenting hound in Britain, generally white or spotted

St Hubert's Hound–black forerunner of the bloodhound

Southern Hound–a heavy, solid English dog

Northern Hound–a lighter, faster hound

Beaver Dog–medieval, possibly like a schnauzer

St John's–small Newfoundland type

Old Water Dog

Poligar–undersized Indian greyhound

Leuvanaar

Devon Staghound

Somerset Harrier

Welsh Hound

Terriers

The Old English terrier was a very fine breed, also the White English terrier. Many of the regional breeds are now either lost, absorbed into other breeds, or very localised–e.g. Paisley, Poltalloch, Devon, Clydesdale, Pittenweem, Aberdeen, Roseneath, Reedwater, Patterdale, Elterwater,

Lancashire, Cheshire etc.

Sheepdogs

Old Welsh Grey

Galway (tricoloured)

Glenwherry of Antrim (marbled)

Lakeland (leggy and shortcoated)

Black-and-Tan

Welsh Hillman (fine red dog, like Alsatian)

Blue Heelers (used at ports for cattle–survive as Australian Cattle dog which is heeler × dingo)

Wheaten Norfolk heeler

Sussex and Dorset bobtails (huge and fierce)

Smithfield sheepdog (briard type)

Drover's Cur (distinct breed of heeler)

Smithfield lurcher (a few still in E England)

Yorkshire and Norfolk heelers

Shooting dogs

Ginger decoy dog or Red decoy dog

Tweed water spaniel

Norfolk retriever

Norfolk spaniel (liver and white)

Land spaniel

Devon and Welsh cockers

Enormous variety of local setter breeds

Dogs with a Past

The late 19th century saw the creation of a great number of new breeds, but some breeds seen today have very long histories indeed, although their modern-day descendants have probably changed to a greater or lesser degree. They include:

The Eastern greyhounds (Saluki, Afghan, Pharaoh hound etc.)

English and Italian greyhounds

Mastiffs

Wolfhounds and deerhounds

Border collie

Dalmatians (originally from India with migrant gypsies)

Bloodhound as descendant of the black-and-tan hound of St Hubert's Monastery in Ardennes (which were bred for over a thousand years)

Small Oriental breeds, many very ancient, e.g. Japanese spaniel, Chinese Happa dog, Pekingese, Tibetan spaniel, Tibetan terrier, Lhasa apso

Chow or Chow chow (2,000 BC at least)

Pug types (at least medieval)

Maltese–one of the oldest breeds in the world; the Roman Emperor Claudius had this type of dog

Many breeds of sheepdog, particularly in Europe

Most spitz-type dogs

Mountain dogs.

Man, Woman & Dog

You ask of my companions. Hills, sir, and the sundown, and a dog as large as myself that my father bought me. They are better than beings, because they know, but do not tell.

Emily Dickinson
You Ask Of My Companions

Royal Dog Owners

Canute–loved hunting with dogs.

Henry II–corgis.

Richard The Lionheart–corgis.

John–often accepted greyhounds in lieu of tax.

Edward III–Irish wolfhounds.

Richard II–greyhound MATHE, deserted him for Bolingbroke.

Henry VIII–Master of Hounds–otterhounds; he also sent four hundred mastiffs to Charles V of Spain as battle and reconnaissance dogs in the war against France.

Mary Queen of Scots–accompanied to scaffold by toy spaniel.

Elizabeth I–her famous pack of singing pocket beagles; she was also Master of Hounds–otterhounds.

William of Orange–life saved in 1572 by little spaniel KUNTZE, or possibly by two Schipperkes.

James I–'six little white earth-dogges' from Argyllshire, presented to King of France.

Prince Rupert–large white poodle BOY or BOYE, which the Roundheads thought had supernatural powers, went with the Cavalry leader everywhere

and was killed at the Battle of Marston Moor on 2 July 1644.

Charles II–dozens of spaniels all his life, bred in his bedroom, overran Hamilton Court and York Palace, always present on State occasions, accompanied him as a fugitive at Carisbrook Castle–hence King Charles Spaniels.

Queen Charlotte, wife of George III–pugs and spaniels.

George IV, as Prince of Wales–pack of dwarf beagles.

Victoria–did much to popularise so many different breeds–see pg 18.

Prince Albert–pack of dwarf beagles, also pointers, dachshunds.

Queen Alexander–bred rough collies, had pekes and Japanese spaniels, a Samoyed called JACKO and a favourite chow called PUNCHY.

Prince George–Newfoundland NELSON and spaniel FLORA.

Princess Alice–SKIPPY, a terrier from Battersea Dogs' Home.

George V–Clumber spaniels at Sandringham as beaters.

Edward VII–as Prince of Wales had many Clumber spaniels, an Irish terrier, and a favourite wire-haired terrier, CAESAR, who slept in his room and who followed his funeral procession; the Prince also exhibited many dogs including greyhounds, deerhounds, bloodhounds and a Tibetan Mastiff called SIRING. As King, he and Queen Alexandra bred basset hounds at Sandringham and dachshunds, and had a red chow with a red tongue. The Queen had a Scottish deerhound, ALEX.

Duke and Duchess of Windsor–pugs.

George VI–bought the corgi ROZAVEL GOLDEN EAGLE for Princesses Elizabeth and Margaret Rose.

Queen Victoria's Dogs

Princess Victoria became the first Patron of the Royal Society for the Prevention of Cruelty to Animals in 1835. She was always surrounded by dogs, and many more were given to her and relegated to her kennels. Favourites were properly buried and given memorials. Apart from her pet dogs named below, she also had plenty of pomeranians, several Italian greyhounds, the first rough collies seen south of the border, a pair of Borzois and some Scottish deerhounds.

DASH or DASHY whom the newly crowned Queen rushed home to bathe immediately after the coronation–buried at Adelaide Cottage with a memorial.

RONA, CAIRNACH and DANDY Skye terriers.

ISLAY terrier.

EOS Prince Albert's Italian greyhound, with a monument at Windsor.

WALDMAN and DACKEL dachshunds.

MARCO red Pomeranian.

BRASSEY black pug.

LOOTIE first Pekingese seen in the west.

LAMBKIN Maltese.

Queen Victoria buried most of her pet dogs in some style. In Windsor Home Park there is an elaborate

Princess Victoria with Eos *by Queen Victoria.*

marble pillar on a granite plinth with the following inscription:

> Here is buried Dackel, the faithful German Dachshund of Queen Victoria, who brought him from Cobury in 1845. Died August 10, 1859. Aged 15 years.

Other Royal and Noble Dogs

Frederick the Great of Prussia—carried an Italian greyhound everywhere with him, even into battle, and he buried it himself, in the Palace garden at Berlin.

Louis XI of France and **Charles I of Lorraine**—passionate hunters with dogs.

Louis XIV—Great Pyrenean court dog known as 'the gentleman with the white fur'.

Louis XV—truffle dogs.

Madame de Pompidou and **Marie Antoinette**—papillons.

12th century King of Ulster—offered six thousand cows for a wolfhound called AIBE and fought a battle when his offer was declined.

15th century King Matthias I—used a Kuvasz for hunting wild boar.

16th century King of Spain—given an Irish wolfhound.

Chinese Emperor AD 565—Persian dog called CH'IN HU or Red Tiger, rode on front of the Emperor's saddle.

King Solomon—Saluki called GIRT IN THE LOINS for coursing.

King Lobengula, 19th century Matabele chief—gave two hundred cattle for one Italian greyhound.

Chief M'tesa of the Waganda, Uganda—described by Capt. Speke as being accompanied by a white dog, a spear, a shield and a woman—the trappings of royalty because eight generations earlier a hunter called Uganda came from Unyoro with a spear, shield, woman and pack of dogs and founded the kingdom of the Waganda.

Great Khan of Tartary—used to hunt with a pack of five thousand dogs.

Dalai Lama in Tibet—exchanged Lhasa apsos for shih-tzus when visiting dignitaries came from China.

Emperors of China—varieties of small spaniels like today's oriental spaniels kept only in the homes of royalty and court nobles; the court dog OKINAMARA had her troubles recorded in Lady Sei Shunagan's *Sketchbook*, AD 991–1000.

Presidential Dogs

George Washington—French staghounds given to him by General Marquis de Lafayette in 1785, with 'voices like the bells of Moscow'.

Abraham Lincoln—his dog had a premonition of his assassination and went berserk at the White House; his sons had a yellow mongrel, FIDO.

Warren G. Harding—LADDIE BOY, Airedale, and OH BOY, white English bulldog.

Calvin Coolidge—DIANA OF WILDWOOD, Shetland sheepdog renamed CALAMITY JANE, an Airedale LADDIE BUCK, half brother of Harding's Laddie Boy and renamed PAUL PRY, a white collie named ROB ROY and a white collie bitch PRUDENCE PRIM.

Herbert Hoover–KING TUT, a police dog.

Franklin D. Roosevelt–FALA, a Scottish terrier, and BLAZE, a bull mastiff belonging to the President's son. In January 1945 Blaze was shipped on an Air Transport Command flight from Washington to Los Angeles and given an 'A' priority rating as a VIP, which meant that three servicemen were denied their places on board and had to hitchhike across the continent. The newspapers, the Republicans and the Senate made a great drama out of the incident. Later that year Blaze had a furious fight with Fala, nearly killing the Scottie, and was put down.

Harry S. Truman–MIKE, Irish setter.

Lyndon B. Johnson–HIM and HER, beagles, BLANCO a white collie, and YUKI the mongrel.

Richard M. Nixon–CHECKERS the Cocker Spaniel and KING TIMAHOE the Irish setter.

Gerald Ford–LIBERTY, golden retriever.

Ronald Reagan–LUCKY, sheepdog.

Famous Dog Owners

Alcibiades' Dog, which had a luxuriant tail, was bought by Alcibiades, an Athenian general who enjoyed shocking people. He promptly docked the dog's beautiful tail so that the public would talk about his latest small act of vandalism rather than about his outrageous past. In the early

1900s there was a sculpture of Alcibiades' dog at Lord Feversham's Duncombe Hall, near Helmsley in Yorkshire: it was very like a Newfoundland.

Bismark, the Iron Chancellor–TYRAS, a Great Dane, his most devoted companion and bodyguard.

Duke of Buccleuch–HECTOR, a Great Dane more than 32 in (81 cm) high.

Bing Crosby and Cindy.

Bing Crosby–CINDY, a black labrador retriever, accompanied Bing to California for the filming of 'Just For You'.

President d'Estaing of France–JUGURTHA, labrador retriever.

Sir Edward Elgar–DAN, an English bulldog belonging to the organist of Hereford Cathedral, may or may not have inspired the *Enigma* Variations when it fell into the river Wye, paddled upstream to regain the bank and, on doing so, barked joyfully. 'Set that to music,' said the organist, and Elgar did so.

Adolf Hitler–BLONDI, an Alsatian, constant companion, was with him in the bunker at Berchtesgarten and was the

The Painter and his Pug *by Hogarth.*

guinea pig to show that the suicidal cyanide capsules worked.

William Hogarth—TRUMP, his favourite pug, which he included in his self-portrait and which everyone claimed resembled him.

Barry Manilow—BAGLE the beagle who was psychoanalyzed.

President Mitterand—NIL, his black labrador retriever.

Isaac Newton—DIAMOND, subject of a doubted story of his dog knocking over a candle and setting fire to a substantial pile of papers that represented years of research.

Charlie Peace—notorious burglar and murderer, always accompanied by his dog which acted as a look-out; after his master was arrested and then

Mick the Miller.

executed, the dog entered Battersea Dogs Home and became a watchdog there for several years.

Stuffed Dogs

BARRY, a famous St Bernard rescue dog who saved more than forty people, the last of whom slashed him with a knife thinking he was being attacked. Barry had to be retired and died in 1815.

BUMMER and LAZARUS, two mongrels who roamed San Francisco with a British eccentric, Joshua Norton (Norton I, Emperor of the United States and Protector of Mexico). Lazarus was run over by a fire truck in 1862 and 10,000 citizens attended his public funeral; Bummer was killed when a drunk kicked him. Both dogs were stuffed and exhibited at the de Young Museum in San Francisco.

A DALMATIAN who was a familiar sight on the London/Brighton coach run was stuffed after his death and displayed in a bar in the Edgware Road.

MICK THE MILLER, the famous greyhound, twice a Derby winner and winner of 19 consecutive races, was later stuffed and displayed in the Natural History Museum, who have a huge collection of stuffed dogs most of which have now been moved to Tring in Hertfordshire.

SEYMOS FRANKLIN was also exhibited at the NHM—he was an Esquimaux dog who died at the age of 12.

Many breeds are on display in the museum at Tring, most of them presented in the first decade or two of this century. They prove how much the breeds have been altered over the years. Some are of particular interest:

TAJEN, Chinese Happa Dog (a breed known since 700 BC)

ROBIN, Toy Trawler spaniel, 'a breed now extinct' (1920) and said to be found chiefly in Holland and Italy; a cross between the curly-coated King Charles spaniels and the old-fashioned curly-coated Sussex spaniel.

LETA OF TAPARAW, a Harlequin Great Dane weighing 140 lbs, (63.5 kg) who won 64 prizes.

FURTHEST NORTH, Eskimo dog, leader of the team taken by Lieutenant Peary across Greenland in 1892 and 1895.

CH. FAIRWEATHER, Old English sheepdog bitch died 1907 and said to be the most celebrated sheepdog of her time.

LUMAN, Saluki belonging to Hon Florence Amherst, obtained from the Chief of the Tahawi tribe in 1897 and one of the original Salukis brought to England.

FULLERTON, English greyhound, winner of Waterloo Cup for four consecutive years (1889–92), sold as a puppy for 850 guineas.

MARQUIS OF LORNE, Scottish deerhound, winner of 30 prizes at the turn of the century.

CH. WANTAGE, basset hound, winner of nine first prizes and 12 second prizes at the turn of the century.

LADY OF THE VALLEY, dachshund, much bigger than present-day breed, with much longer legs, generally less exaggerated and more attractive.

WHINLANDS TORNADO, Dobermann pinscher used as a demonstration animal while it was alive (died 1969) for lectures at the British Museum.

AFRICAN HAIRLESS DOG, a little known rare breed also called Abyssinian Sand Terrier.

RUSSIAN LAP DOG, only four inches long and perhaps three inches high, with white wavy coat.

MEXICAN LAP DOG about five or six inches long, with white fluffy coat.

OLD-FASHIONED BULL TERRIER–the original fighting bull terrier, much rounder face than the modern Staffordshire breed.

TOY BULL TERRIER–only 46 registered with the Kennel Club in 1968.

TIBETAN DOG, a very pretty crossbreed–sire a Tibetan Spaniel, dam a Lhasa terrier.

Frozen Pets

Taxidermy is not good enough for Californians. When a pet dies in the Sunshine State it can now be freeze-dried and displayed in its grieving owner's living-room. TASHA is a freeze-dried Pekingese which died in 1983 and which now sleeps peacefully and permanently on a coffee table in San Francisco Bay. The cost? $400 for a small dog, $1,000 for a German shepherd dog, $1,500 for a pit bull terrier.

Edible Dogs

Sandwich (!) Islanders used to eat dogs, but were so fond of them when they were alive that a man would sooner resent an injury to his dog than to his child. They treated their dogs better than their children, carrying them in their arms when they came to muddy or rough places on their travels.

Tierro Del Fuegians used to have small fox-like domesticated dogs which were exceptionally crafty fishing and hunting aids. As a shoal approached land, the dogs swam out and drove them into nets or shallow creeks. They also caught sleeping birds and brought them back to their masters, all so silently that they could return for more birds because none were disturbed. Their masters neglected and ill-treated them, rarely feeding them and leaving them to forage or catch their own fish, but the dogs were watchful and very faithful. Despite the neglectful attitude, the Fuegian had great respect and even affection for his dog: he would sooner eat one of the old women than the dog, because the dog was useful to him!

The Jelly Dog–another name for the beagle

Plum-Pudding Dog–the dalmatian

Salty Dog–cocktail: 1½ msrs vodka or gin; grapefruit juice, teasp. salt. Put ice cubes in tumbler, add vodka, top up with grapefruit juice and add salt

Sausage Dog–dachshund; field spaniel; basset; Dandie dinmont; drever; lhasa apso; Skye terrier (longest and lowest terrier)

Hot Dog–frankfurter in a long roll

Dog in a Blanket–roly-poly pudding

Dog's Body–pease pudding

Dog's Dinner/Breakfast–anything very untidy

Dog's Paste–sausage or mincemeat

Dog's Vomit–meat and biscuit hash

Dog's Nose–gin and beer

Dog's Soup–water

And of course **The Hair of the Dog**–a stiff drink the morning after a hard night's drinking to help alleviate a hangover. Originates from Ancient Rome where, if bitten by a dog, the Romans would down a concoction containing a burnt hair from that canine to ward off any ill effects.

Scottie from *Lady and the Tramp*.

Dog-owners and Dog food

*Old Mother Hubbard went to the
cupboard,
To find her poor dog a bone,
But when she got there the
cupboard was bare,
So the poor little doggy had
none.*

Consumption of Dog food in Britain

	Tons	Worth
1979	484,000	£222 million
1980	434,000	£239 million
1981	467,000	£264 million
1982	495,000	£284 million
1983	573,000	£343 million
1984	621,000	£380 million
1985	658,000	£411.5 million

Of all dog owners, 90 per cent feed prepared pet foods to their dogs at least once a week.

The inventor of a long-standing cheap and popular brand of tinned dog food used to eat his product for breakfast to show just how wholesome it was.

Raymond A. Sokolov, in 'Man Bites Dog Foods and Finds Some to His Liking', tells of 'one 4-year-old Saluki bitch and one 31-year-old male food editor' who decided to undertake a genuine consumer test of various American dog foods. Both of them starved themselves for sixteen hours before the tasting session began.

The Saluki, Cleo, however hungry she might have been by then, absolutely refused to touch the first two dishes, which were of the dry-food type, but she devoured everything else with great and indiscriminate enthusiasm–raw minced beef, chicken and liver flavoured tinned dog meats, dog biscuits, horsemeat, offal or whatever. She then had a good doze.

The editor approached his tasting rather more warily and methodically, very conscious of appearance, smell, taste and texture. He awarded stars to each dish, ranging from four for dog food that could be compared with human food to nil for something so foul it made him retch. Nutritional value was not taken into account. Here are his considered comments:

*** **Minced Raw Beef** Approve–but needs seasoning.

*** **Milk-Bone Biscuit** Tasty enough to eat two, the second with butter. Could replace Ry-Krisp.

** **'Prime', Chicken Flavour** Moist, sweet, yellow cubes. No chicken flavour. Surprising resemblance to sweet Passover cake.

** **'Medallion' Beef-Flavoured Chunks** Strong meat flavour; texture like cake.

* **'Purina' Dog Chow** (dry food) Stale biscuit texture; subtle meat flavour. Agree with Cleo.

* **'Recipe' Beef & Egg Dinner** Excellent smell, like chop-suey, but no taste. Mushy texture like cold-cream. No seasoning.

* **'Laddie Boy' Lamb Chunks** Best smell of all, but disappointingly no taste at all. Gooey texture.

'Top Choice' Chopped Burger Most unpleasant taste. Drastic red colouring.

Rubbery texture, pasty in mouth.

'Gaines' Meal (dry food) Concretised sawdust. Cleo even more right on this one.

'Alpo' Horsemeat Chunks Looks awful, smells like stew, tastes foul.

Unrated
'Daily All-Breed', Liver Flavour Inexpensive homogenised food. Brown-green in colour. Similar in effect to ipecac, a purgative South American shrub! Strong, mysterious smell. Couldn't get it down therefore couldn't rate it. The dog liked it, though.

Dog Ownership Profile, 1985

Total dog population: 6.3 million

Total households with dogs: 5.0 million
  One dog only–83 per cent
  More than one dog–16 per cent

Most common type of home: Detached, semi-detached or terraced, notably in rural areas

Area of densest dog ownership: Midlands and North
Age group of highest level of ownership: 35–54

Socio-economic breakdown:

Group	All households	Dog-owning households
AB	15%	15%
C1	24%	22%
C2	28%	33%
DE	33%	30%

Most Popular Breeds in 1985

German shepherd dog

Labrador retriever
Yorkshire terrier
Jack Russell terrier
(All information courtesy of PFMA.)

Dog Disorders

They say a reasonable amount o' fleas is good fer a dog–keeps him from broodin' over bein' a dog, mebbe.

Edward Noyce Westcott
David Harum

Achondroplasia (dwarfism) bulldog, dachshund, basset

Acute Bloat boxer, deerhound, Great Dane, Irish setter, Irish wolfhound, mastiff, St Bernard

Blindness (various forms) Alaskan malamute, boxer, collie, German shepherd dog, Irish setter, labrador retriever, poodle

Eye/Eyelid Disorders American cocker spaniel, bloodhound, Boston terrier, bulldog, chow, Pekingese, St Bernard, shar-pei, spaniels (several), wire-haired fox terrier. (Collies and dalmatians may show heterochromia, i.e. different colours in the same iris)

Distemper Eskimo dog and Japanese spaniel particularly prone

Epilepsy American cocker spaniel, beagle, boxer, poodle

Hydrocephaly (water on the brain) American cocker spaniel

Infectious Abortion beagles in kennels

Rheumatism/Arthritis boxer, cocker spaniel, dachshund, German shepherd dog, Great Dane, St Bernard

Skin Problems lots of dogs,

especially miniature black and tan terriers and pomeranians

Stomach Problems Boston terrier, boxer and mastiff have weak stomach acids; small spitzes need careful feeding.

Most Common Problems Encountered at PDSA Clinics

Aston
Skin
Ears
Distemper/Parvovirus

Brighton
Fleas
Ears
Diarrhoea

Bristol
Skin
Gastro-enteritis
Chest complaints

Glasgow
Distemper/Parvovirus
Gastro-enteritis
Skin complaints and ears

Hull
Distemper/Parvovirus and skin complaints
Road accidents
Allergies, eyes, ears

Leicester
Digestive problems/Parvovirus
Skin complaints
Road accidents

Liverpool
Vomiting and diarrhoea
Fleas
Road accidents

Manchester
Parvovirus
Fleas and skin
Ears

Wimbledon
Skin
Ears
Heart

Dogs in Law

The Foo Dog or Buddhist Lion Dog was an imaginary 'keeper of the Jewel of Law', usually portrayed in porcelain or wood with a ball under one foot. It has a lion's mane, shaggy tail, and a head like a Pekingese.

9th century Dog Laws
Alfred the Great 'taught even falconers and dogkeepers their business' and made laws specifying compensation if bitten by a dog. Welsh laws of the same period mention three kinds of Cur (Mastiff, House Cur, Shepherd's Cur).

10th century Dog Laws
Howel the Good (Hywel Dada) of S Wales made numerous references to dogs in his laws, including big dun-coloured hounds, greyhounds, spaniels and harriers. A king's buckhound or covert-hound was valued at one pound and a greyhound at six-score pence. In 1080 and 1180 a greyhound was worth half a buckhound.

11th century Dog Laws
'No mean person may keep greyhounds.' Before the time of the Magna Carta, the punishment for destroying a greyhound was the same as that for murdering a man.

The Forest Laws of Henry II
Only the privileged few could keep greyhounds or spaniels in the royal forests. Farmers and substantial freeholders could keep mastiffs for the defence of their homes, but only if the dogs were disabled so that they could not chase and seize deer.

Shogun Tsunayoshi, the 'Dog Shogun' of the late 17th century, passed a law that all dogs must be addressed politely and treated kindly. He ended up caring for a hundred thousand dogs himself, at the expense of the Exchequer. The resulting inflation brought about the introduction of an unpopular tax on farmers.

Church and Monastery Dogs

Saintly Connections

St Bernard The Hospice du Grand Saint Bernard, one of the highest human habitations in Europe, was originally the site of a temple to Jupiter. Bernard of Menthon rebuilt it as a refuge offering hospitality to pilgrims, and it was here that the well-known breed of large mountain dogs was developed to help guide travellers on their way.

St Benignus and **St Wendelin** In medieval art a dog represented fidelity. Each of these saints is portrayed with a dog at his feet.

St Dominic A dog is often portrayed carrying a lighted torch to guide St Dominic.

St Hubert The patron saint of hunters gave his name to one of the early breeds of hound. St Hubert was a passionate deer hunter but he never hunted again after he beheld the apparition of a stag with an image of Christ on the cross between its antlers.

St Roch St Roch's dog was the epitome of faithfulness. The saint was smitten with the plague while he was tending victims of that terrible disease; he took refuge in the depths of the forest, and the dog brought him his daily bread and licked his plague sores.

Church-going Dogs

In the 14th century, nuns in Romsey often took hounds and other pets with them into church services. William of Wykeham had to reprove them, saying, 'We have convinced ourselves by clear proof that some of the nuns bring with them to church birds, rabbits, hounds and suchlike things, whereunto they give more heed than to the offices of the church.'

The Bishop of Gloucester was officiating at a service at the Abbey Church in Bath one Sunday with the usual assortment of medieval dogs in attendance. Some of them were turnspit mongrels, accompanying their cooks. The lesson was from Ezekiel, and it included the words, 'As if a wheel had been in the midst of a wheel.' To the turnspits 'wheel' was a strong reminder of hard work, and 'they all clapt their Tails between their Legs and ran out of the Church'.

For several centuries thereafter dogs were commonly used in church as foot-warmers for the congregation. Special dog-minders were employed to keep them under control with 'dog nawpers'. In 1636 the Bishop of Norwich had special rails and pillars built to keep the dogs away from the Communion bread.

Superstitions

Discord The Greeks thought that if a stone which had been bitten by a dog was dropped into wine, those who drank the wine would fall out amongst themselves.

Docking Two thousand years ago docking a dog's tail was thought to prevent madness. The practice was encouraged in more recent history by taxation (a bob-tailed dog was a working dog).

Howling It is a widespread superstition that dogs howl when there has been a death. To quote Longfellow:
In the rabbinical book it saith
The dogs howl when, with icy breath,
Great Sammael, the angel of death,
Takes thro' the town his flight.

Mandrakes In medieval bestiary, the only way to capture a mandrake root (to which all sorts of magical powers were attributed) was by using a wolfhound to tear it from the earth.

Omens An ancient Kaffir superstition was that bad luck should be expected if a dog leaped on to the roof of a hut. The Damara of south west Africa dreaded meeting a dog with one foot like that of an ostrich—a sure sign of impending death.

clothing by 18th century Siberians, and the coat clippings of Tibetan terriers used to be mixed with yak hair and woven into a soft, semi-waterproof cloth. Wool from poodles, Old English sheepdogs etc., is sometimes spun and knitted by enthusiasts.

Glove/Pocket Beagle A very small dog from Elizabethan times up to the 19th century, said to be small enough to be carried in a lady's glove; but in fact the term applied to any beagle under ten inches high.

Muff Dog Toy terrier small enough to slip into a muff and keep its owner's hands warm.

Powderpuff In hairless breeds, the occasional pup which is born with normal hair and teeth.

Pyjama Dog Afghan hounds have been called 'greyhounds in pyjamas'.

Sleeve Dog Japanese spaniels and Chinese temple dogs, carried in the loose sleeves of oriental gowns.

Water-Rugs Shakespeare's description of the dog he used for hunting waterfowl on the river Avon, probably an English water spaniel.

Clothes Dogs

Comforter Small spaniels were used to cure human disorders; 'comforters' were pressed against the afflicted part, keeping it warm and sometimes effecting a cure simply because the patient believed it was possible.

Dog Fur is generally thought much too inferior to be worn, except perhaps as a travel rug. But samoyed skins were worn as

Expensive Dogs

Hath a dog money? Is it possible A cur can lend three thousand ducats?

Shakespeare
The Merchant of Venice

The first dog ever to be sold for as much as a £1,000 was a rough collie. A Mr Megson in the 1880s was always willing to pay well for good collies and he gave record prices of £1,005 and £1,300.

Two of the Duchess of Marlborough's Dogs *by John Wootton*.

£1,500 was considered an 'enormous sum' paid for a collie in 1900. Other prices of the year include £1,000 for a bulldog and £500 for fox terriers 'was not uncommon', but the best gundogs only fetched two or three hundred pounds.

The Duke of Northumberland offered 'Piper' Allen a farm for a Dandie Dinmont called HITCHEM. Allen spurned the offer, saying, 'I wadna take yer hale grund fer him.'

£63,800 was paid in 1985 for a cast-iron table supported by four gilded life-size deerhounds.

£143,000 was paid through Sotheby's for a painting of a spaniel and foxhound belonging to the Duchess of Marlborough, who wrote, 'I am very fond of my three dogs, they have all of them gratitude, wit, and good sense, things very rare in this country. They are fond of going out with me: but when I reason with them, and tell them it is not proper, they submit, and watch for my coming home, and meet me with as much joy as if I had never given them good advice.'

Dogs' Bodies

British organisations concerned solely or partly with dogs include:

The Battersea Dogs' Home, founded 1860 at Holloway

Lesley Scott Ordish with her English Setters Lady, Fant and Poppy.

The Guide Dogs for the Blind Association, founded 1934

Hearing Dogs for the Deaf, introduced under the auspices of the Royal National Institute for the Deaf in 1982. Now a separate charity in its own right to assist people who suffer loss of hearing by training dogs to respond to everyday sounds

Joint Advisory Committee on Pets in Society (Jacopis), 1974

The National Canine Defence League

NGRC Retired Greyhound Trust, established 1974

The People's Dispensary for Sick Animals, founded 1917

PRO-Dogs Charity, founded 1976 by Lesley Scott Ordish

PRO-Dogs Active Therapy (PAT) Scheme, 1983 involves volunteers, all of whom are members of PRO-Dogs, taking their registered PAT dogs to visit hospitals, hospices and homes for disabled, children and the elderly

Better British Breeders, register of caring dog breeders to ensure responsible dog breeding, 1986

The Royal Society for the Prevention of Cruelty to Animals, founded 1824 (the world's oldest animal welfare organisation)

And in Japan:

Jaws is the Japanese Animal Welfare Society, founded in the 1950s by Lady Gascoigne, wife of the then British Ambassador in Tokyo.

Mrs Michiko Fujita, an estate agent by day and a geisha by night, has five hundred stray dogs in her Tokyo home. Food and helpers' salaries cost her more than £10,000 a month and she was helped by the 500 members of the Fujita BOW-MEIOW ASSOCIATION. The money recently ran out but the animals were saved by a donation of 37 tons of tinned pet food from a French company.

The Battersea Dogs' Home

It all began in the early summer of 1860 when Mrs Mary Tealby, a widow, visited her friend Mrs Major in Canonbury Square, Islington, and was taken to the kitchen to see a small, filthy, worn-out dog in the last stages of starvation. Mrs Major had found it in the street, in an age when there were thousands of neglected dogs roaming the city. The two women began nursing the pathetic bundle and collected several more waifs over the next few days.

On 2nd October that year, with the help of Mrs Tealby's brother, they published a prospectus appealing for funds to care for more dogs. In November they held a first committee meeting in the Pall Mall offices of the Royal Society for Prevention of Cruelty to Animals, which had been established in 1824. The Dogs' Home was housed in Holloway, and the cover of their first report made this plea:

'The Committee would willingly hope and believe that no one who is capable of appreciating the faithful, affectionate, and devoted nature of the dog, can have seen any of these intelligent creatures lost, emaciated and even dying from starvation, without feeling an earnest wish that there were some means established for rescuing them from so dreadful a death, and restoring them to usefulness.'

Ten years later, the Home moved to Battersea, where it still is today.

James Pavitt was the first keeper: he came to Holloway in 1860 and stayed with his dogs until he died in 1883. His original procedures are still the pattern for today. Each new arrival was given a traditional English name like Fido or Spot, and a number, which was attached to its collar and entered into the register. Then the dog was given its own

place, depending on its health and temperament—perhaps a basket or box, or a cage. Much the same happens today, except that they long ago used up all the names!

From its small and humble beginnings in a kitchen in Islington, the Battersea Dogs' Home has become world famous and given food and shelter to more than 2.5 million dogs.

At the end of every annual report of the Battersea Dogs' Home are quoted these lines penned by Byron, a great dog lover:

With eye upraised, his master's look to scan,
The joy, the solace, and the aid of man;
The rich man's guardian and the poor man's friend,
The only creature faithful to the end.

Some Famous Battersea Dogs

Lady Gloria Cottesloe, wife of the present Chairman of The Battersea Dogs' Home, describes many of the refuge's past inmates in her book *The Story of The Battersea Dogs' Home* (published by David & Charles). Here are some of them:

A hundred working sledge dogs sent by Sir Ernest Shackleton from Canada. They were to accompany him on his second Antarctic Expedition, arranged just before World War I broke out, and they were kennelled at the Home's Hackbridge annex free of charge for two months. They were all half-breeds—husky-collie, husky-St Bernard, and husky-wolf crosses.

Two Airedales from the Home

were the first of Britain's fully trained war dogs in World War I. Edward Richardson eventually set up a War Dog School at Shoeburyness in 1916 and most of his recruits came from Battersea. Airedales were found to be ideal– they adapted to any climate, they were strong with great stamina, and were highly trainable. Their main job was as messengers, making their way across areas where no man could have escaped being killed or injured.

AIREDALE JACK was one who received a posthumous VC, for example. The Battersea war dogs also included collies, sheepdogs, whippets, retrievers and deerhounds for messenger work and sentry duties, and mastiffs, boarhounds and German shepherd dogs for guard duties. Another important aspect of their war work was with the Red Cross as ambulance dogs. Some 7,000 British dogs were killed in action during World War I, and many more died subsequently from wounds or the effects of gas. Nearly all of them were from Homes, and most of them were Battersea dogs.

Seven Airedales and Seven Alsatians were recruited from the Home during World War II by an RAF Commandant as sentries for his station–their meat ration was as much as any man's. Although it was thought that dogs would not be so useful in World War II, in fact they were essential. British dogs were trained to guard vital points against airborne attacks, track down landed parachutists, lay wires under fire, carry ammunition and poison-gas canisters, sniff out enemy positions, and do Red Cross and

liaison work. There was a big demand for dogs 'of a sombre colour, one-and-a-half to two-and-a-half feet at the shoulder, able to carry loads of at least half their own weight', and the Airedales and German shepherd dogs from Battersea fitted the specification perfectly. A few years after the war, in 1952, British Road Services came to Battersea for dogs to guard their marshalling yards and depots.

Not all the Home's dogs were war heroes! Many caught the eye of famous people, like:

Lupino Lane, the famous acrobat and songster (he of 'The Lambeth Walk') who chose a male bull terrier and was somewhat startled when it gave birth to puppies even before he reached home.

Cherry Kearton, the well-known photographer and big-game hunter of the 1920s, who chose fox terrier PIP as his companion for an African safari; Pip proved to be so outstandingly brave that he was awarded a lion's mane by tribesmen.

Gracie Fields, who borrowed some Battersea dogs in 1932 to make her film *Look On The Bright Side*, and could not bear to return a big Airedale that became devoted to her.

Tommy Steele, who was reunited with his lost family pet, TRAMP, at the Home.

Lloyd George, whose St Bernard RIFFEL spent its quarantine at Battersea when it came to England from Switzerland. Riffel caused havoc when his six months were over and he moved into prime ministerial mansions. *The Sun* reported:

'Riffel, the Premier's St Bernard

dog, left Chequers today, and the staff at Downing Street is still busy mending the carpets and putting the furniture back where it came from. He stayed only about twelve hours at No 10 but it was quite enough; and on the advice of a consulting architect it was decided to move him into larger premises at once. Otherwise the Coalition headquarters might have collapsed and brought the Government and the Foreign Office down with it.'

But only a few of the Battersea dogs caught the eye of the famous. Most of them became the devoted companions of everyday people:

THE FOX TERRIER who lived for nine years under the Judges' Triangle at the Law Courts; the Home eventually persuaded her to move into a nice family house in Hendon, and it was then found that she had accumulated two hundredweight of bones in her judicial lair.

THE MUSICAL DOG whose new owner had to give up playing Liszt rhapsodies because they made the dog howl; it loved only Chopin, whose music soothed it so much that it became motionless and wore a silly grin on its face.

THE FOXHOUNDS that got carried away on the scent and ended up at Battersea: one (Old Berkshire) found its way seventy miles from Abingdon to Mitcham; another (Old Surrey & Burstow) travelled from East Grinstead to Wallington; a third (Surrey Union) was lost from Earlswood Common and ended up three weeks later in Bromley, Kent. These were all in the 1920s, and as hounds are earmarked the Home could return them immediately to their appropriate packs.

FLORRIE was a mongrel who lived with George Clark, an ex-serviceman who put his head in the gas oven and died a pauper. She guarded his body and twice escaped from the police station to return to his room. On the day George was buried, Florrie was found a comfortable new home in Chelsea.

OAK TOP was a famous greyhound who was stolen from Catford Stadium kennels. The thieves dyed him ginger but abandoned him when the dye began to run. Not long after, a very streaky greyhound turned up at the Home.

SANDY was a member of the Tailwaggers Club; he and his owner managed to enrol nearly thirteen hundred new club members, and they also raised enough money to subsidise more than a hundred dog licences for those who could not afford them. Later they raised another £60, in shillings, for a guide dog for the blind.

MARGARET and another stray found themselves among the very select few: they were chosen as pets for wealthy sheikhs and were whisked to their new homes in private jets.

LADDIE was a ten-year-old collie who left Battersea to join SHAGGY the 'hopeless sheepdog', FLASH the mongrel who kept running away, and STEVIE the poodle who failed as a pet. The foursome became a road safety demonstration team with the Canine Defence League and travelled more than 15,000 miles each year to schools and children's cinema clubs.

ENOCH was another pampered ex-Home mongrel: he was given his own Italian nanny in 1957, and he was often dressed up in a white cotton suit with a tartan bow-tie and a pocket handkerchief. He was given a party by his doting mistress on his eleventh birthday—all his friends came to help demolish the blue-iced cake.

PETER AND PAUL were two black labradors. Peter was blind and Paul was his self-taught guide dog, carefully steering him past all obstacles when they first came to the Home. Luckily their arrival was given plenty of newspaper coverage and their owner quickly found them again.

DOLORES became a star in her own right, out-acting Rod Steiger in *Across the Bridge*. The mongrel was described in the *News Chronicle* as 'one of the most endearing bitches in screen history—a mournfully unthoroughbred spaniel . . . who was discovered in Battersea Dogs' Home. St Sebastian never gazed skyward with so monumental a look of martyrdom as Dolores in her final anguish. Landseer never found a sitter whose nose was more moist with devotion.'

BOOTSIE was found on Charing Cross station guarding a pair of shoes, from which he refused to be parted at Battersea and even at his new home in Bristol.

CHINA perhaps epitomises the joy and companionship so many people have found with their Battersea dogs. In 1982 two people visited the Home looking for a dog—female, not too big, and in desperate need of love and attention. 'We found her in N.23—a pathetically disinterested dog, not long lost her pups. Her only acknowledgement of our interest was to snarl at us. She'd obviously had it very rough and wasn't prepared to trust anyone. She had a few health problems which didn't help, but her worst problem was her refusal to respond to friendly advances with anything but a fairly aggressive snap.' But they took her home all the same, and now they are 'the proud owners of the toast of the local woods. The day's high spots are the twice daily squirrel chases round the woods which brings the place to a halt, especially when she runs up the trees after them! It's not unusual for her to be 12–15 feet up in a tree, sitting on the branches, awaiting an unwary squirrel. She doesn't catch them!'

Most commonly received breeds, 1985

1	Mongrels	15,128
2	German shepherd	11,162
3	Jack Russell type	577
4	Labrador	334
5	Collies (all types)	297
6	Dobermann pinscher	292
7	Greyhound	209
8	Spaniel (all types)	187
9	Yorkshire terrier	154
10	Lurcher	131
11	Bull terrier	103
12	Poodle	96
13	Irish setter	78
14	Boxer	71
15	Old English sheepdog	57

Least common (1 only)
Bichon frise
Briard
Griffon
Groenendael
Keeshond
Kerry Blue
Lakeland terrier
Manchester terrier

Miniature pinscher
Newfoundland

Total dogs received:	20,542
Total dogs sold:	18,396
(average price £12.34)	
Total dogs claimed:	2,871
(average price £4.78)	
Total destroyed:	8,721
Total visitors:	67,689

Guide Dogs

*My guide, and mine own
familiar friend.*

Psalm 55

During World War I a German
doctor noticed that an alsatian
was very caring towards a blind
patient, and he began
experimental training to see if
dogs could be used as guides for
the blind. Mrs Dorothy Harrison
Eustis, a wealthy American who
bred alsatians, saw the German
training centre and wrote about it.
Morris Frank, a blind American,
was inspired by her article and
contacted Mrs Eustis, who then
set up L'Oeil Qui Voit in Vevey,
Switzerland (1928) and also
established the first guide dog
school in the United States. Morris
Frank was the first guide-dog
owner in America, with his famous
BUDDY. In England Mrs Muriel
Crooke, a dog breeder and trainer
in Liverpool, and Mrs Rosamund
Bond, a breeder and exhibitor of
alsatians, met Mrs Eustis and then
began their own British training
classes at Wallasey. The classes
eventually led to the formation of
the Guide Dogs for the Blind
Association in this country.

First units trained (1931)
– all German shepherd dogs:

FLASH and Allen Cadwell
META and G. W. Lamb
JUDY and Musgrave Frankland

FOLLY and Thomas Ap Rhys

1985 Guide Dog statistics

Guide dog ownership	3,650
Breeding stock	252
Puppies at walk	820
Under training	683
Teams trained:	
new owners	600
replacements	314
Retired	500
Number of training centres	7
Voluntary fund-raising	
branches	374

Breeds used	Approx. % of total
Labrador retrievers	50%
Labrador × golden retrievers	25%
Golden retrievers	12%
German shepherd dogs	12%

The remainder are mostly collie
types.

RSPCA Dogs

1985 Dog facts

Number of new homes found for dogs	51,778
Convictions for cruelty to dogs	992
Disqualification orders	511
Humane destructions	52,089

Medal winner
The Margaret Wheatley Cross for
PC John Gordon, victim of the
Harrods bombing who, though
very seriously injured himself,
thought first of his dying dog.

PDSA Dogs

Analysis of breeds attending
centres in 1985
Aston
Collie/labrador cross
Alsatian
Dobermann and Staffordshire bull
terrier

Golden Retriever guide dog being worked.

Brighton
Mongrel
Yorkshire terrier
Poodle

Bristol
Collie/labrador cross
Terrier cross
Dobermann/alsatian, Irish setter

Glasgow
Alsatian
Labrador
Collie cross, West Highland and
   Cairn terrier

Hull
Alsatian
Yorkshire terrier
Mongrel and Jack Russells

Leicester
Collie/alsatian cross
Terrier type
Jack Russell

Liverpool
Mongrels
Alsatian
Dobermann, Staffordshire bull
terrier

Manchester
Mongrel

Alsatian
Dobermann, Yorkshire terrier

Wimbledon
Collie/alsatian cross
Alsatian
Jack Russell.

Jobs for Dogs

Postal Dogs were employed in teams to draw the Sussex mail between Steyning and Storrington within the living memory of a Findon man who died in 1931 at the age of 95 (Cannon Palmer, rector of Sullington). Teams of dogs were also used to take fish from Southampton to London, two or four dogs drawing a cart with the driver sitting with his legs on the shaft. They were often Newfoundlands, and four could pull a load of three or four hundredweight of fish. And in the 1820s long teams of dogs would pull the travelling shows which visited country fairs. Before the use of draught dogs was banned in this country in 1856 (more

RAF sniffer dogs and their handlers.

because of the noise they made and encouraged than because of any concern about cruelty to dogs) they were commonly seen pulling carts for bakers, butchers, knife-grinders, hawkers and so on.

Butter churning

Curing indigestion (living hot-water bottles)

Detecting drugs. Four breeds trained at the RAF at Newton to detect dangerous drugs are: labrador, Sussex spaniel, German short-haired pointer and border collie (see below left). These stalwart dogs are used by H.M. Customs and Excise, U.S. Air Force and the Royal Navy

Detecting gas leaks

Drawing off parasites from their masters

Fostering anything from tiger cubs to chicks and piglets

Keeping railway lines free of wandering sheep

Turning mill wheels, meat spits and prayer wheels

Warming the feet of church-goers.

The Dogs of War

Caesar's spirit, ranging for revenge,
With Ate by his side, come hot from hell,
Shall in these confines, with a monarch's voice,
Cry, 'Havoc!' and let slip the dogs of War.

Shakespeare
Julius Caesar

Dogs have been used in battle since ancient times and many became war heroes and mascots.

Assyrian attack dogs were shown in a Pergamon frieze of 280 BC.

Herodotus describes a battle where men fought men, horses fought horses, and dogs fought dogs.

British Mastiffs were exported in considerable numbers to Rome and Gaul for battle work; they usually wore armour.

Rottweilers were used by the Romans, at first to herd 'meat on the hoof' for the soldiers, and later as aggressors. The Romans also used Pyrenean and Bernese mountain dogs.

Henry VIII sent mastiffs to Charles V of Spain for his French war, as war dogs and for reconnaissance.

Elizabeth I's soldiers used hundreds of dogs against the Irish rebels.

In World War I dogs were used extensively by several armies, for Red Cross work and as messengers, draft dogs and sentries.
Germany had 6,000 trained German shepherd dogs ready and waiting before 1914 and sent 20,000 to the battlefront.
France used briards extensively. 10,000 dogs were sent to the battlefront to locate wounded for the Red Cross, to act as front-line sentries, and to carry ammunition in back-packs. They also used 8,000 sledge dogs in the Vosges Mountains.
Britain also used thousands of dogs, many from Battersea Dogs' Home, and 7,000 were killed in action.

In World War II dogs were used again in very large numbers.

America used dogs to search for wounded in the jungles of the Pacific arena and to flush out snipers.

Britain had a War Dog School at Shoeburyness.

Germany used 200,000 dogs, mostly to guard concentration camps.

In Norway the Defence Minister is empowered to mobilise all privately owned Norwegian Elkhounds in case of war–they are highly prized as sledge dogs.

War Heroes

BILLY, brindled bull terrier with Royal Ulster Rifles 1900, Transvaal. Wounded, and later learned to feign a limp for a ride (it was a mounted infantry company).

BOB, terrier with Scots Guards in Crimean War, who chased Russian cannon-balls when they fell in British lines, often still hot.

BOBBY, small white rough-haired terrier born in Malta, with Royal Berkshire Regiment during the Second Afghan War. In July 1880 at the battle of Maiward the 2nd Battalion was reduced to 11 men and Bobby, and eventually only Bobby, who was then taken prisoner. Later presented to Queen Victoria in a red coat; she awarded him the Afghan Medal.

BOXER, black-and-tan terrier with South Staffordshires in Malta in 1882 who always 'saluted' officers. Fell out of train window en route to Gordon Relief Column in Egypt.

CHIPS, collie/husky/German shepherd mixture, was the first American dog to be sent overseas in World War II with the army's newly formed K-9(!) Corps. He was later awarded the Purple Heart and Silver Star but the honours were taken away from him because it was deemed inappropriate to commend an animal.

CRIB, bull terrier with The Buffs in the Peninsular War. Fought a battle with a poodle from the French lines: they met in No Man's Land and Crib killed the poodle. He died aged 18 in 1830 and was buried at St Martins in the Strand.

DASH, retriever with Royal Engineers, severely wounded in China War.

DICK, the famous fox terrier of Rorke's Drift, 1879 Zulu War. Painted by A. de Neuville.

DRUMMER JACK, black and white fox terrier with Coldstream Guards who served on front line throughout World War I. Wore ribbon of 1914 Star, Victory Medal and General Service Medal, and after the war always accompanied Drum Major Murrell when he mounted guard at Buckingham Palace.

An ENGLISH BULLDOG working for America was decorated with five ribbons and a Bronze Star for war work. Another was promoted to Corporal.

JACK, Airedale, posthumous VC.

JEAN, pretty spaniel/collie mongrel with Black Watch, serving in Mesopotamia, Egypt, Palestine and Syria, 1916–18.

JOCK, mongrel with Black Watch throughout Egyptian Campaigns. Wounded at El Teb and Kirbekan, died 1891. Medal with five bars and Egyptian Star.

PINCHER, small smooth terrier attached himself to Black Watch

on way home from Peninsular War, 1814. Saw action at Quatre Bras (severely wounded but would not quit the field) and Waterloo. Shot by a keeper when chasing a rabbit in Scotland.

SCOUT, an Irish terrier with the Royal Dragoons in the South African War of 1899–1902, who eventually led her troops into Bloemfontein when peace was declared. Awarded Queen's Medal with six bars and King's Medal with two bars. Died in India.

SMOKEY, Yorkshire terrier found in a shellhole and used to haul telegraph wires in inaccessible places.

SNOB, brindle and white mongrel terrier in the Crimean War. Awarded Crimean Medal with Alma Clasp.

VERDUN BELLE, mongrel at Verdun, 1918, who located the wounded marine she had adopted.

William the Hun guarding the hatch.

'WILLIAM THE HUN', a bull terrier of the British Flotilla Leader, SWIFT. William saw three actions and had three plates on his collar inscribed: Jutland, 31 May 1916; Channel Raid, 1916; Channel Raid, 21 October 1917.

Mascots

BEVERLEY, St Bernard with E. Yorkshire Regiment, 1947, beautifully dressed in tasselled maroon coat.

THE BOXER, large dog with Royal Ulster Rifles 1st Battalion from 1893. Truculent, would fight any dog he saw.

BRAGGS, one of many Great Dane mascots of the Gloucestershire Regiment (called The Old Braggs after a Colonel of the Regiment). BRAGGS I was born in 1925; he was succeeded by BRAGGS II etc.

BRIAN BORU, Irish wolfhound named after famous romantic King of Ireland. Presented to Irish Guards by Irish Kennel Club in 1902.

DOG AND MONKEY were the regimental mascots of the 8th Canadian (Winnipeg) Battalion. Photograph (right) taken near. Aberle, 25 May 1916.

FLAMBEAU, French dog-postman, delivered mail between Lanslebourg and Fort de Solieres (height 2,700 m) for eight years to 1937 for 92nd Alpine Light Infantry. Always got through, even if men could not, and was only living contact between the fort and the valley. Retired 1937 but became homesick for the snow and the Fort and made his own way back the following year. He died the day after he reached the Fort, in front of the assembled platoon.

FRENCH POODLES were the mascots of 19th century German students.

FRITZ, St Bernard adopted by Royal Hampshire Regiment: he had been seen roaming when the regiment attacked Arromanches in 1944 and later appeared with the first batch of German officer prisoners in England.

GEORGE TIREBITER, irritable Airedale cross who chased cars. Mascot of University of Southern California's football team, the Trojans, from 1940. Stolen before UCLA-USC game in 1947 and shaved so that the remaining coat formed letters U C L A.

HANDSOME DAN, the original

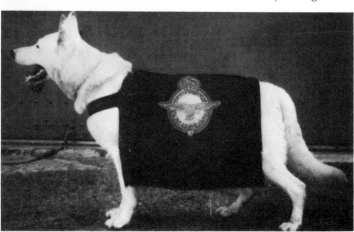

Storm.

Yale bulldog mascot from 1889 for ten years, also a prize-winning show dog.

NORWICH TERRIERS became the mascots of Cambridge University students.

SAM, Newfoundland with The Prince of Wales's Leinster Regiment (Royal Canadians). He was one of the first to enlist when the Regiment was raised in 1858. Died after a musket bullet wound turned septic. His coat was then tanned and turned into an apron for the big drummer.

STORM, pure white alsatian with dark eyes, born in 1944. RAF Police Dog Training Centre instruction dog in demonstrations and parades at Netheravon. Paraded in ceremonial uniform. Demonstrated police dog skills to other dogs, who learned by observation.

THRUPPENCE, mongrel listed on inventory board when Seaforth Highlanders took over duties from 1st Battalion The Durham Light Infantry at the Waterworks, Yangtzepoo, Shanghai, in 1938. Named as successor to previous mascot, Tuppence, and also called Cheefo, Sausage, Stupid and Jimmy. Liked the mess wine waiter and music.

UGA I, II and III, white English bulldog mascots of the University of Georgia's football team.

WALLACE, large shaggy St Bernard with The Canadian Scottish Regiment (Princess Mary's) from 1940. Much loved by the men who tried to smuggle him into Scotland by drugging and crating him. His box went over the side in the ship's cargo net but hit the dockside and exposed the half-awake dog, who howled. Band started up to drown the noise. Unfortunately as there was a dock strike he could not be unloaded and hidden, and was found by Immigration, who put him in quarantine.

Canadian mascots.

WATCHMAN, white bull terrier presented 1949 to Territorial Army as the prize in an Infantry competition. Ranked as Sergeant, and made life-long member of the Tailwaggers Club.

Medal Winners

RATS, the famous Jack Russell terrier adopted by the Welsh Guards serving in Crossmaglen, received the PRO Dogs Gold Medal in 1979.

MACHERI, a poodle who died while trying to rescue its owner from a fire, was given the Stillman Award in 1984.

NACHO, a chihuahua who was killed by burglars while protecting its owners, received the Stillman Award in 1985.

ZORRO, German shepherd, awarded a gold medal as the Ken-L-Ration Dog Hero of the Year in 1975 for rescuing and protecting his unconscious master in the Sierra Nevadas.

The National Canine Defence League

Has been awarding medals to dogs and to humans for services to dogs since 1891. Many of the dogs were commended for giving warning of fire. Others were awarded for acts of great bravery or for saving lives. Some of the more unusual or outstanding medallists are:

BESS, an Airedale in Northumberland, saved three children from being run down by a train.

BORIS, an alsatian from Streatham Common on holiday with his master in Devon, became marooned with his master on a rock cut off by the tide. A rescue party failed to fling a rope across to the rock, and Boris plunged into the raging sea, swam to the cliff, seized the rope and returned to his master.

BRANDY, a golden retriever trained by the RAF as a drug detector, who made 27 detections on a short secondment to the United States Air Force. In 1977 he joined H.M. Customs & Excise and retired in 1982 at the age of 10 having made 160 finds totalling

Brandy.

4,040 kilograms of cannabis worth more than £4 million.

JACKIE, a Glaswegian alsatian, rescued his master who was being savaged by another alsatian.

JOLLY, a three-year-old collie who found an unconscious man under the snow.

REX, a collie from Hull, who three times saved the life of an accident-prone little boy (on a busy road, from a pond, and from a railway line).

ROUGH, a Yorkshire sheepdog, kept an infuriated bull at bay so that his injured master could crawl to safety. Several other dogs have been commended over the years for saving their owners from bulls and even from angry horses.

TIPPER, a collie whose howl brought his master out of a coma in hospital and saved his life.

People Power

The National Canine Defence League's Silver Medals awarded to humans 'for gallant acts on behalf of dogs' have included these heroines and heroes:

Barbara Boyle, aged 17, of St Anne's-on-Sea who at grave risk to herself rescued no less than fifteen dogs from burning kennels.

George Carlow, aged 18, of St Mary Cray who descended fifty feet down a dene hole to rescue a dog. The soil at the edges of the hole was loose and threatened to collapse at any moment.

Eliza Chown of Bethnal Green for entering a burning house and rescuing her dog. Mrs Chown was severely burned and spent some time in hospital.

Harold Cornford, aged 18, of Newhaven, who dived into the sea from a breakwater to rescue a dog.

Edward Crump, aged 84, of Worcester, who rescued a dog from the River Severn.

Mavis Donoghue of Cookham who rescued her servant, her two dogs and her canaries when the hotel of which she was manageress caught fire.

Clifford Gray of Everton, aged 16, who saved a dog from the Leeds–Liverpool Canal.

Marion Hannan of Bradford, Yorks, for rescuing a dog from a fire at a post-office.

Malcolm Alexander Macleod, aged 10, of Isle of Lewis, who attempted to rescue his collie which had fallen through the ice on a river. Sadly Malcolm lost his life in the attempt.

Ronald Narramore, aged 12, of Golders Green who rescued a cocker spaniel from a burning kitchen at home.

Thomas Sach of Chelmsford, aged 10, who entered the River Cann to rescue a dog which had fallen through the ice.

Christopher Tugby of Oakthorpe, an elderly man who saved a drowning alsatian from a river on a dark winter's night.

Marjorie Wood from Northam in Devon who rescued a drowning elkhound from a fast flowing river in pitch darkness.

The 1985 PRO-Dogs Medals

CHITA, German shepherd belonging to the author Joyce Stranger, became the one thousandth dog to be registered for the canine hospital visiting

The Brown Dog memorial.

programme, known as P.A.T. (PRO-Dogs Active Therapy).

NIPPER, for rescuing 300 sheep during a farm fire and, although his paws were burnt, returning to fetch out the cows.

OSCAR, pet of the year for raising money for new equipment for a children's hospital where he brought a child out of a coma.

TOBY, for sniffing out a gas leak on an estate.

Monuments and Memorials

But the poor dog, in life the firmest friend,
The first to welcome, foremost to defend . . .
Lord Byron
Inscription on a Newfoundland Dog

BALTO, black malamute who delivered serum to Nome, Alaska.

BARRY, St Bernard, Paris (saved

46

44 from snow, killed by 45th).

BETH GELERT, fictitious deerhound, North Wales.

BOATSWAIN, Lord Byron's Newfoundland (lengthy eulogy).

THE BROWN DOG memorial in Battersea in memory of the Brown Dog antivivisection riots of 1906. The new statue was unveiled on 12 December 1985.

CARLOS, retriever, Gujarat (Afghanistan campaign).

THE DOG was Diogenes (412–323 BC). The young king of Macedonia went to see the philosopher and introduced himself, saying, 'I am Alexander, surnamed the Great.' Diogenes replied, 'And I am Diogenes, surnamed the Dog.' When he died the Athenians put up a marble memorial pillar with a dog on top.

GREYFRIARS BOBBY, Skye terrier, Edinburgh.

HACHIKO was an exceptionally loyal akita which used to meet its master's train every evening at Tokyo's Shibuya station. His master died suddenly but Hachiko continued to meet the train for the next nine years in case he returned. Local commuters kept him well fed. His statue now stands outside the station.

JOCK OF THE BUSHVELD has a road named after him in Transvaal.

EDWARD LAVERACK, who made English setters famous, is buried in the Shropshire village of Ash. His tombstone bears the image of one of his dogs along with the following inscription: To the memory of Edward Laverack; born Keswick, 1800; died at Broughall Cottage, 1871. This monument was erected by

Greyfriars Bobby.

admirers in England and America.

MAIDA was Sir Walter Scott's very famous deerhound, the prototype for Bevis and Roswal in Scott's novels. He 'died quietly in his straw, after a good supper' in October 1824 and was buried beneath a mound at Abbotsford, marked by a carved likeness.

OLD DRUM was a black-and-tan farm hound which was shot by a neighbour who was then sued for damages by the hound's owner. During the subsequent trial, lawyer Graham Vest gave a moving peroration on the bond between men and dogs, reducing the entire court-room to tears. The 400-word text of the eulogy is reproduced beneath a bronze statue of Old Drum in Courthouse Square at Warrensburg, Missouri, and it refers to '... the one absolutely unselfish friend that a man can have in this selfish world, the one that never deserts him and the one that never proves ungrateful or treacherous ... faithful and true even to death'.

RINGWOOD, otterhound, by the river Cherwell at Venus Valley.

A STANDARD SCHNAUZER, Stuttgart statue with watchman.

National Dogs

British Bulldog

Boston Terrier An American dog with French and English blood being a cross of the bulldog, French Bulldog, bull terrier and boxer. First shown in Boston in 1870

Finnish Spitz Ubiquitous in Finland but rare elsewhere

French Poodle

Hungarian Vizsla.

Hungarian Vizsla Hungary's most famous hunting dog

Japanese Akita By government decree, every champion Akita is declared a National Art Treasure and made a ward of the government

Ch. Traza Teasel, Keeshond.

Keeshond Dutch symbol of resistance. Cornelis 'Kees' de Gyselaer was leader of the Patriots Party; the established Orangists had the PUG as their symbol

Kerry Blue As Irish as the shamrock

Russian Spitz or Laika A very common breed in the USSR, and it was one of these who became the first dog in space.

There are probably between 120 million and 150 million dogs in the world. Here is where some of them live:

United States	35 million
France	8 million
Britain	6 million
Germany	6 million
Italy	4 million
Belgium	1 million

and the

Japan Kennel Club registers about three and a half million pedigree dogs.

The Dog Shows

When They Began

1859 **Newcastle-upon-Tyne**–
the first dog show ever
held. It was open only to
pointers and setters; 60
dogs were shown and the
prizes were Pape's sporting
guns (local gunmaker Mr
Pape was joint sponsor of
the show with Mr
Shorthose).

Other British shows
followed in the same year:

Birmingham–classes for
pointers, English and Irish
setters, retrievers, Clumber
spaniels. It was so
successful that a National
Dog Show Society was
established for the purpose
of holding a show of
sporting dogs at
Birmingham every winter.

Cleveland–the Cleveland
Agricultural Society
established a show for
foxhounds at Redcar.

Edinburgh

1865 **Southill**, Bedfordshire–
first Working Trials of
pointers and setters held
on the estate of Mr S.
Whitbread, M.P.

1865 **Paris Show**

1870 **Exhibition** arranged
under the management of
Messrs G. Nutt, S. E. Shirley
(founder of the English
Kennel Club) and J. H.
Murchison. It made a heavy
loss.

1875 **First American Shows**

1877 **First Westminster Dog**
Show, New York. By 1906
there were 1,956 dogs on
show at the Westminster in
Madison Square Gardens.

1886 **Allied Terrier Club**
Show–the first to be
managed by Charles Cruft
in Britain. The son of a
jeweller, Cruft joined
James Spratt's new
business selling 'dog cakes'
(made from ship's biscuits)
in Holborn in 1876. In 1878
he undertook the
promotion of the canine
section in the Paris
Exhibition.

1891 **Crufts Show**–the first of a
long series. Cruft booked
the Royal Agricultural Hall,
Islington, and he continued
to run financially
successful shows until he
died in 1938.

1948 **Kennel Club/Crufts**
Show–held at Olympia, the
first Crufts Show under the
jurisdiction of the Kennel
Club.

1905 British Show Entries

Kennel Club Show	–1,789
Crufts Dog Show	–1,768
Ladies Kennel Association	–1,306
Manchester	–1,190
Edinburgh	– 896
Birmingham	– 892

The Clubs

There are national kennel clubs all
over the world, and many of them
came into existence towards the
end of the 19th century.

1776 **The First Club**–Lord
Orford of Marham Smeeth,
near the Norfolk town of
Swaffenham, set up a

greyhound coursing club. Its membership was restricted to the number of letters in the alphabet.

1873 English Kennel Club–40 breeds and varieties recognised; the first volume of the *Kennel Club Stud Book* was published the following year.

1884 American Kennel Club– took over from an earlier club set up in 1878. The first dog registered was an English setter, ADONIS.

1886 New Zealand Kennel Club

1888 Canadian Kennel Club– first dog registered was another English setter, FOREST FERN.

1889 Finnish and Swedish Kennel Club

1895 Ladies Kennel Association–an English breakaway formed because women were not admitted to the Kennel Club.

1897 Danish Kennel Club

1898 United Kennel Club of America

1898 Norwegian Kennel Club

1898 Italian Kennel Club

1912 Spanish Kennel Club

1931 Portuguese Kennel Club

1953 Scandinavian Kennel Union

1958 Australian National Kennel Council

After the first organised dog show at Newcastle-upon-Tyne in 1859 (pointers and setters only), the fashion for shows was set and there were two a year for the next ten years. By 1870 it was felt that a controlling body was needed. The Crystal Palace Show was first held in that year by the National Dog Club, whose committee was subsequently called together by Mr S. E. Shirley, M.P., of Ettington. As a result of that meeting, twelve gentlemen got together on 4th April 1873 and founded the Kennel Club. They began a Stud Book, edited by Mr Frank Pearce, and its first volume contained the records of shows from 1859. They also formulated a code of ten rules relating to dog shows, and undertook to 'recognise' any society which adopted the code for its shows, the winners of which would be eligible for the Stud Book. The Stud Book has been published annually since then, and the Kennel Gazette has been published as a monthly since 1880.

In 1880 the Club introduced a system of reserving the use of a name for a specific dog to avoid duplication in the Stud Book– until then there had been a plethora of dogs called Spot, Jet, Bob, Vic, Bang, Nettle and so on. In 1898 the Rules disbarred ear-cropping, and crop-eared dogs have been ineligible for competition ever since in this country. In 1981 a computer was installed to process Kennel Club registrations, which currently average about 175,000 a year. Today the Club is concerned not just with the shows and pedigrees but with a wide range of canine matters. Its main objective, however, is still to improve pure-bred dogs.

Growth of the English Kennel Club Registrations

1900	11,650
1910	18,918
1920	16,819
1930	48,784
1940	13,968 (World War II)
1950	100,433
1960	133,618
1970	180,000
1980	201,614

Breed Societies Registered with the Kennel Club

In the last twenty years, the number of dog shows held each year in this country has increased by fifty per cent. In 1984, for example, there were about seven thousand shows of all types, including nearly five hundred Championship shows. There are more than six hundred societies recognised for individual breeds; some of the breeds have only one or two societies, but some have considerably more. The breeds with the most breed societies are:

47	German shepherd dog (Alsatian)
23	Cocker spaniel
20	Bulldog
18	Dachshund
18	Pekingese
17	Poodle
15	Staffordshire bull terrier
15	Collie
14	Boxer
13	Welsh corgi (Pembrokeshire)

American Kennel Club—First-of-Breed Registrations, 1878/1885

	Reg No.	Name	Breed
1878	1	ADONIS	English setter
	534	ADMIRAL	Irish setter
	793	BANK	Gordon setter
	1187	ACE OF SPADES	Pointer
	1352	BOB	Irish water spaniel
	1353	BUSTLER	Clumber spaniel
	1354	CAPTAIN	Cocker spaniel
	1363	JACK (alias TOBY)	Sussex spaniel
	1408	SUNDAY	Chesapeake Bay retriever
1885	3188	BLUNDER	Beagle
	3223	DASH	Dachshund
	3234	BOUNCER	Basset hound
	3236	JOLLY	Harrier
	3237	CARSDOC	Bloodhound
	3241	BARON WALKEEN	Greyhound
	3249	BLACK SHEP	Collie
	3271	BAYARD	Mastiff
	3280	CHIEF	St Bernard
	3286	GEORGE	Pug
	3289	CRICKET	Fox terrier
	3306	AILEEN	Irish terrier
	3307	BELLE	Yorkshire terrier
	3308	NELLIE II	Bull terrier
	3310	PRINCE CHARLIE	Scottish terrier

Most Recent First-of-Breed Registrations

1980	GLEN IRIS BOOMERANG	Australian Cattle Dog
1979	BAR SINISTER LITTLE RUFFIAN	Norfolk terrier
1978	ASUNCION	Ibizan hound
1976	CANNAMOOR CATINKA	Bearded collie
1973	HOLMENOCKS GRAMACHREE	Soft-coated wheaten terrier
1973	AMANDA LAMLEH OF KALIA	Tibetan terrier
1972	AKITA TANI'S TERUKOSHI	Akita
1972	SHA-BOB'S NICE GIRL MISSY	Bichon frise
1969	CHOO LANG OF TELOTA	Shih-tzu

Breeders who Created or Rescued a Breed

4th Duke Alexander of Richmond & Gordon–Gordon setter

'Piper' Allen–Bedlington and Dandie Dinmont terriers

Lady Florence Amherst–Saluki

Grand Duke Karl August–Weimeraner

Emanuele Boulet–soft-coated griffon

Captain Brownrigg and the **Earl of Essex**–shih-tzu

Sir Edward Chichester–Finnish spitz

Captain Darby and **Dr Keul**–bouvier des Flandres

Duke of Devonshire–mastiff (Lukey)

Louis Dobermann–Dobermann pinscher

Gamekeeper Dupuy–braque Dupuy

Captain John Owen Tucker Edwards–Sealyham terrier

Oswalde Aranha Filho–Brazilian tracker

Mr Fuller–Sussex spaniel

Lord Galway–basset hound

Baron Girard–beagle harrier

Duke of Gloucester and **Lady Stradbroke**–Australian terrier

Captain Graham–Irish wolfhound

A P Hamilton–Hamilton hound (Hamiltonstovare)

Holland-Hibbert (3rd Viscount Knutsford)–labrador retriever

Franta Horak–Bohemian terrier

Lady Howe–labrador retriever

John Hulme–Manchester terrier

Jones Family of Ynysfor–Welsh terrier

Eduard Korthals–wire-haired pointing griffon

Edward Laverack and **Purcell Llewellin**–English setter

Matgo Law–shar-pei

'Doggy' Lawrence–Norwich terrier

Legh Family–mastiff (Lyme Hall)

Duncan McNeil (Lord Colonsey)–deerhound

Malcolms of Portalloch–West Highland white terrier

Earl of Malmesbury–labrador retriever

Dignity and Impudence *by Sir Edwin Landseer.*

Sir Dudley Marjoribanks–golden retriever

Bernard of Menthen–St Bernard

Dukes of Newcastle and Noailles–Clumber spaniel

Duchess of Newcastle–borzoi

Lady Helen Nutting and **Veronica Tudor Williams**–basenji

Jonathan Plott–Plott hound

Captain Renssens–schipperke

Frederick Roberth–German spaniel

Rev. John Russell–Jack Russell terrier

Squire Trevelyan–Bedlington terrier

Col. Hayden Trigg–Trigg hound.

Mrs Cruft with H. S. Lloyd and prize-winning spaniel, Tracey, Witch of Ware (1948).

Well-bred Dogs

Men are generally more careful of the breed of their horses and dogs than of their children.

William Penn
Reflexions and Maxims

The matter becomes serious when fashion begins to dictate to the poor dog what he has got to look like, and there is no single breed of dog the originally excellent mental qualities of which have not been completely destroyed as a result of having become 'fashionable'.

Konrad Lorenz
Man Meets Dog

Charles Cruft, son of a jeweller, left Birkbeck College in 1876 and joined James Spratt, who was selling his new 'dog cakes' in Holborn. (Dog cakes were invented in the United States after someone successfully disposed of a consignment of ship's biscuits to dog owners.) From office boy, Cruft was promoted to travelling salesman, visiting all the large sporting estates in this country, and later on the Continent as well. In 1886 he was asked to manage the Allied Terrier Club Show at Westminster's Royal Aquarium and in 1891 he booked the Royal Agricultural Hall at Islington for his first Crufts Show. Thereafter he made quite a financial success of his shows, which he ran annually until his death in 1939. His widow continued to organise the show for a few years until in 1948 the first Crufts Show under Kennel Club jurisdiction was held at Olympia. It was moved to Earls Court in 1979 and extended to three days in 1982. The 90th Show was held in February 1986.

Crufts Roll of Honour

Since 1928 an annual award has been given to the Best in Show at Crufts. The award was continued when the Kennel Club took over the organisation of the show in 1948, apart from breaks in 1949 and 1954. The following breeds have won this top accolade most often:

6 Cocker Spaniel—and all of them H. S. Lloyd's dogs: LUCKYSTAR OF WARE won in 1930 and 1931; EXQUISITE MODEL OF WARE in 1938 and 1939; TRACEY WITCH OF WARE in 1948 and 1950.

3 Labrador Retriever—all from Lorna Countess Howe: BRAMSHAW BOB in 1932 and 1933; CH CHEVERALLA BEN OF BANCHORY in 1937.

3 Greyhound—PRIMELEY SCEPTRE (1928); SOUTHBALL MOONSTONE (1934); TREETOPS GOLDEN FALCON (1956)

3 Wire-Haired Fox Terrier–

CH CRACKWYN COCKSPUR
(1962); CH BROOKEWIRE
BRANDY OF LAYVEN (1975);
CH HARROWHILL
HUNTSMAN (1978)

3 **German Shepherd Dog**–CH
FENTON OF KENTWOOD
(1965); CH HENDRAWEN'S
NIBELUNG OF CHARAVIGNE
(1969); CH RAMACON
SWASHBUCKLER (1971)

2 **Pointer**–PENNINE PRIMA
DONNA (1935); CH CHIMING
BELLS (1958)

2 **Welsh Terrier**–TWYNSTAR
DYMA-FI (1951); CH
SANDSTORM SARACEN
(1959)

2 **Standard Poodle**–CH
TZIGANE AGGRI OF
NASHEND (1955); CH
MONTRAVIA TOMMY-GUN
(1985)

2 **Toy Poodle**–OAKINGTON
PUCKSHIL AMBER
SUNBLUSH (1966); CH
GRAYCO HAZLENUT (1982)

2 **Lakeland Terrier**–
ROGERHOLM RECRUIT
(1963); CH STINGRAY OF
DERRYABAH (1967)

2 **English Setter**–SH CH
SILBURY SOAMES OF
MADAVALE (1964);
BOURNEHOUSE DANCING
MASTER (1977).

Winners for last ten years

**1977 Bournehouse Dancing
Master** (English setter)

1978 Harrowhill Huntsman
(Wire-haired fox terrier)

1979 Callaghan of Leander
(Kerry blue terrier)

1980 Shargleam Blackcap
(Flat-coated retriever)

1981 Astley's Portia of Rua
(Irish setter)

1982 Grayco Hazlenut (toy
poodle)

**1983 Montravia Kaskarak
Hitari** (Afghan hound)

**1984 Saxonsprings
Hackensack** (Lhasa apso)

1985 Montravia Tommy-Gun
(standard poodle)

1986 Ginger Xmas Carol
(Airedale terrier).

Kennel Club Registrations: Top Three

Only 10 breeds have been
represented in the top three for
Kennel Club registrations from
1932 to 1984:

Cocker Spaniel (1st: 19 years;
2nd: 5 years)

German Shepherd Dog (1st: 14;
2nd: 16; 3rd: 10)

Miniature Poodle (1st: 11; 2nd:
1; 3rd: 2)

Yorkshire Terrier (1st: 6; 2nd: 3;
3rd: 8)

Wire-Haired Fox Terrier (1st:
3; 2nd: 10; 3rd: 4)

Labrador Retriever (2nd: 10;
3rd: 9)

Pembroke Welsh Corgi.

Pembroke Welsh Corgi (2nd: 5;
3rd: 1)

Toy Poodle (2nd: 3; 3rd: 3)
Scottish Terrier (3rd: 11)
Pekingese (3rd: 4)

Kennel Club Top Ten Breeds Registered

The top 10 breeds for 1983 were also the top 10 (in the same order) for 1984:

	1983	*1985*
German Shepherd Dog	20,593	21,649
Labrador Retriever	14,016	15,156
Yorkshire Terrier	12,407	12,141
Golden Retriever	10,270	11,451
Cavalier King Charles	9,978	10,090
Dobermann Pinscher	8,499	9,953
Cocker Spaniel	8,064	7,619
Rottweiler		6,836
English Springer Spaniel	6,825	6,666
Rough Collie	5,572	
Staffs Bull Terrier	4,709	6,419

Over the last twenty years there seems to have been a trend towards bigger and more powerful breeds, particularly the guard dog types such as German shepherds and Dobermanns. Comparisons between 1964 and 1985 reveal some dramatic changes in popularity:

UP	*1964*	*1985*
Bearded Collie	121	1,443
Dobermann Pinscher	875	9,953
Field Spaniel	5	85
Gordon Setter	60	586
Lhasa Apso	115	1,404

Newfoundland	25	655
Old English Sheepdog	310	1,958

Ch. Chesara, Rottweiler.

Rottweiler	0	6,836
Tibetan Terrier	57	601
Weimeraner	127	1,070

DOWN		
Basset Hound	1,529	737
Cardigan Welsh Corgi	240	139
Miniature Poodle	13,246	1,475
Miniature Smooth Dachshund	2,828	915
Pembroke Welsh Corgi	6,310	1,297
Sealyham Terrier	784	63

Kabaroin Black Diamond, Smooth Dachshund.

Smooth Dachshund	2,292	303
Toy Poodle	10,572	2,740

Kennel Club Bottom of the League, 1984

Several breeds registered no dogs at all in 1984: most of these were newly recognised that year. Some, however, had been previously registered, including the following.

American Water Spaniel
(12 in 1981)

Australian Kelpie
(5 in 1981)

Hungarian Kuvasz
(1 in 1979)

Pomeranian.

Komondors.

Komondor
(5 in 1983, 1 in 1982, 9 in 1981, 15 in 1979)

Neapolitan Mastiff
(9 in 1983, 1 in 1982, 1981 and 1980, and 8 in 1979)

Small Munsterland
(last registration: 1 in 1981)

Tibetan Mastiff
(13 in 1983, 2 in 1982 and 1981, 7 in 1980).

Pop Dogs in Britain in 1903

Fox Terrier most popular of all breeds, on the streets and at shows

Rough Collie neck and neck with the fox terrier for years

Irish Terrier second most popular terrier

Airedale third most popular terrier

Bulldog one of the most popular dogs, and increasingly so

Pomeranian probably the most popular toy breed

Labrador Retriever described as 'never popular'

Pekingese 'not extensively known as yet'

Chihuahua very scarce in 1898 but by 1903 it was seen now and again at the shows.

Some Stars of the Breeds

Afghan Hound ZARDIN, the sensation of 1907

Alaskan Malamute GRIPP OF YUKON, the first champion

Basenji FULA

Basset Hound BASALT and BALLE, 1866

Bedlington Terrier OLD FLINT, 1782

Belgian Sheepdog DUC, sensation of 1898

Borzoi CH. CASPIN, who stood at 34.5 in

Bulldog ROSE and CRIB, painted by Abraham Cooper

Chesapeake Bay Retriever SAILOR (red) and CANTON (black), the original shipwrecked founders of the breed (1807)

Chihuahua MIDGET, the first registered by the AKC (1904)

Clydesdale Terrier BLYTHSWOOD PEARL, 1891, 40 firsts

Cocker Spaniel OBO, an English dog whelped 1879, and his son OBO II, were the founders of all today's cockers, English and American

Collie (Bearded) JEANNIE OF BOTHKENNAR, 1944, forebear of all modern winners

Dandie Dinmont HITCHEM, the first

Dobermann Pinscher LUX, LANDGRAF, RAMBO and the very ferocious SCHNUPP, the four original dogs bred by German tax collector Louis Dobermann at Apolda, Thueringia, to protect him from bandits in the 1880s

English Setter PONTO and MOLL, bred by Edward Laverack in 1825

Fox Terrier OLD JOCK, OLD TRAP and TARTAR, exhibited at Birmingham in 1863–all modern fox terriers (smooth and wire-haired) trace back to these three dogs

Golden Retriever: NOUS, the original yellow offspring of a black flat-coated retriever, bred to a Tweed spaniel to produce four

founders of the breed, CROCUS, PRIMROSE, COWSLIP and ADA

Gordon Setter DANDY, won the setter prize in the world's first dog show at Newcastle-upon-Tyne in 1859

Great Dane HECTOR, SATAN and PROSPERINA–all giants

Iceland Dog CHUCK, first English registration, 1905

Italian Greyhound GOWAN'S BILLY, 1859

Kerry Blue MARTELL'S SAPPHIRE BEAUTY, first champion, 1920

Labrador Retriever CH BANCHORY BOB, Crufts Best in Show 1933 and 1934 (and could have been in 1932 and 1935)

Lakeland Terrier CH STINGRAY OF DERRYABAH, 1964 Crufts Supreme Champion

Newfoundland OOLUM, the black 'bear dog' taken by Lief Ericson to Newfoundland in 1000 AD

Old English Mastiff TURK, huge and famous winner, 1870s

St Bernard TELL, famous in 1860s; PLINLIMMON at the turn of the century; FLORENTIUS, winner of more than a hundred first prizes; BARRY I (born 1854), father of the English St Bernards

Schipperke TIP, first dog registered with St Huberts, 1882; stolen by the crew on voyage to Britain and sold in New York

Siberian Husky BOSS, 10 years as team leader, immense courage and strength; retired to live with an adoring Frenchwoman and died of soft living two years later after getting slightly damp in a shower of rain one night

Smooth Fox Terrier CH

WARREN REMEDY, Best in Show at Westminster 1907–1909

Welsh Corgi (Pembroke) ROZAVEL RED DRAGON, born tailless, great progenitor of the breed.

Giants

By height

Irish wolfhound
(31 in–39½ in/79 cm–100 cm)

Great Dane
(30 in–41½ in/76 cm–105 cm)

Mastiff
(30 in upwards/76 cm)

Scottish deerhound
(30 in upwards/76 cm)

Tibetan mastiff
(28 in upwards/71 cm)

Borzoi
(28 in–31 in/71 cm–79 cm)

Greyhound
(28 in–30 in/71 cm–77 cm)

Tallest living dog.

Newfoundland
(28 in on average/71 cm)

Pyrenean mountain dog
(27 in–32 in/69 cm–81 cm)

Afghan hound
(27 in–29 in/69 cm–74 cm)

Komondor
(26 in–31 in/66 cm–79 cm)

Fila Brasileiro.

Fila Brasileiro
(26 in–30 in/66 cm–76 cm)

By weight

St Bernard
(record weight 310 lb/140.6 kg)

Tibetan mastiff
(record 220 lb/99.8 kg)

Mastiff
(175 lb–190 lb/79.4 kg–86.2 kg)

Newfoundland
(120 lb–155 lb/54.4 kg–70.3 kg)

Great Dane
(minimum 120 lb/54.4 kg, 132 lb/59.9 kg in USA)

Irish wolfhound
(minimum 120 lb/54.4 kg)

Bull mastiff
(110 lb–130 lb/49.9 kg–60 kg)

Pyrenean mountain dog
(100 lb–155 lb/45.4 kg–70.3 kg)

Komondor
(up to 125 lb/56.7 kg)

Bloodhound
(90 lb–110 lb/40.8 kg–49.9 kg)

Dwarves

By height

Chinese Imperial Ch'in.

Chinese Imperial Ch'in
(3 in–6 in/7.6 cm–15 cm)

Chihuahua
(6 in–9 in/15 cm–23 cm)

Pekingese
(6 in–9 in/15 cm–23 cm)

Miniature smooth-haired dachshund
(7 in–8 in/18 cm–20 cm)

Belgian griffon
(7 in–8 in/18 cm–20 cm)

Italian greyhound
(less than 8 in/20 cm)

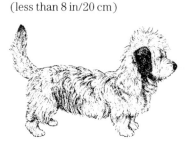

Dandie dinmont.

Dandie dinmont
(8 in–11 in/20 cm–28 cm)

Papillon
(8 in–11 in/20 cm–28 cm)

Bichon frise
(8 in–12 in/20 cm–30 cm)

Little lion dog
(8 in–14 in/20 cm–36 cm)

Shortest recorded dog is a
Yorkshire Terrier, $2\frac{1}{2}$ in/6.3 cm.

By weight

Chinese Imperial Ch'in
(1.5 lb–5 lb/0.7 kg–2.3 kg)

*Ch Anyako Admiral, Long-haired
Chihuahua.*

Chihuahua
(2 lb–6 lb/1.9 kg–2.7 kg)

Pomeranian
(from 3 lb/1.4 kg)

Griffon bruxellois
(3 lb–10 lb/1.4 kg–4.5 kg)

Toy fox terrier
(3.5 lb–7 lb/1.6 kg–3.2 kg)

Little lion dog
(4.5 lb–9 lb/2.0 kg–4.1 kg)

Phalene
(5 lb–10 lb/2.3 kg–4.5 kg)

Maltese
(less than 7 lb/3.2 kg)

Yorkshire terrier
(less than 7 lb/3.2 kg–smallest on
record is 4 oz/113 g)

Pekingese
(7 lb–11 lb/3.2 kg–5 kg)

Well Coated

There are plenty of shaggy breeds and several are particularly prized for the length and beauty of their coats.

Long Coats on Little Dogs

Clydesdale terrier
(11 in/28 cm on either side of body)

Maltese
(8.5 in/22 cm)

Silky terrier
(5–6 in/12–15 cm)

Yorkshire terrier

Bichon avanese

Bichon frise

Shih-tzu.

Shih-tzu

Phalene

Pekingese

Chinese Imperial Ch'in

Lhasa Apso

Dandie dinmont

Shaggy Coats

Briard

Bouvier des Ardennes

Griffons (various)

Bergamasco

Old English sheepdog

Pumi

Bearded collie

Tibetan terrier

Pyrenean sheepdog

Curly Coats

American water spaniel

Irish water spaniel

Bedlington terrier.

Bedlington terrier

Curly-coated retriever

Poodle

Portuguese water dog

Puli

Corded Coats

Komondor
(8–11 in/20–28 cm long)

Puli

Waterproof Coats

Water spaniels (various)

Newfoundland

Otterhound (very oily)

Retrievers (various)

Eskimo dog

Keeshond

Leonberger

Spinone Italiano

Boykin spaniel

Hairless Dogs

African sand dog

Chinese crested

Mexican hairless or
Xoloitzcuintli

Turkish naked dog

Rampur dog of India

Abyssinian hairless dog

Barbary dog

Spots, Splodges and Speckles

African hairless dogs

Australian cattle dog

Blue and red tick coonhounds

Braques (various)

Canaan dog

Catahoula leopard dog

Chinese crested

Clumber spaniel (freckles)

Dalmatian

English setter

Harlequin Great Dane

Munsterlander

Norrbottenspets

Pointers and spaniels (lots)

Odd Colours

Blue

Kerry Blue

Bleu de Gascogne

Red

Irish setter

Irish terrier

Redbone coonhound

Yellow

Vizsla (dark sand)

Clumber spaniel (white and lemon)

Chocolate and Liver

American water spaniel

Australian kelpie

Dachshund

Flat-coated retriever

German pointer

Irish water spaniel

Sussex spaniel (rich golden liver)

Chestnut and Tan

Pharaoh hound

Pudelpointer

Soft-coated griffon

Gleamers

Porcelaine

Welsh springer spaniel

Very Individual

Irish water spaniel (puce)

Weimeraner (elephant grey)

Hairpieces

Beards and Moustaches

Bearded collie

Bouviers

Briard

Briard and friend.

Kerry blue terrier

Lhasa apso and shih-tzu

Little lion dog

Maltese

Poodle

Schnauzers

Terriers and wire-haired breeds

Wolfhounds and deerhounds

Topknots

Afghan

Australian terrier

Briard

Ch. Jaspar of Kojak, Chinese crested.

Chinese crested

Dandie dinmont

Irish water spaniel

Maltese

Mexican hairless

Poodle

Shih-tzu

Silky terrier

Yorkshire terrier

Eyebrows and Fringes

Bearded collie

Cairn terrier

German wire-haired pointer

Irish wolfhound

Otterhound

Poodle

Schnauzers

Silky terrier

Tibetan, Yorkshire and Welsh terriers

Wire-haired dachshund

Face Facts

Eyes

'In sporting dogs,' says Drury, 'eye colour is indicative of character and temperament. Go for full dark hazel. Avoid small eyes, particularly of light yellow–they are usually wild harum scarums, very difficult to train or control though often good workers.'

Amber, Gold and Yellow Eyes

Afghan hound

Brittany spaniel

Chesapeake Bay retriever

Clumber spaniel

Corgi (Cardigan)

Fila brasileira

Ibizan and Pharaoh hounds

Pudelpointer

Weimeraner

Spectacles

Dandie dinmont

Keeshond

Hypnotic Eye

Border collie

Blue Eyes

Corgi (Cardigan merle)

Kelpie

Siberian husky

Weimeraner

Wall or China Eyes

Old English sheepdog

Smooth collie

Mouthfuls

Black/Purple Tongue is seen only in the **chow** and **shar-pei**.

Hairlessness in a breed is genetically sex linked to missing teeth and sometimes missing toenails.

Shar-peis have curved scimitar-like canines for fighting.

Pekingese teeth need frequent cleaning to avoid premature loss.

Lhasa Apsos are prone to teeth problems.

SNOWBIRD was an **Alaskan malamute** who had a tooth problem. A dentist gave him a gold tooth, and thereafter he was called GOLDFANG.

Long Ears

Bassets have been described as dogs whose ears sweep the morning dew

Bloodhound pups sometimes trip over their own ears

Dachshund

Otterhound

Otterhound.

Many other hounds have very long ears indeed, particularly the continental varieties.

Spaniels, like the cocker and King Charles

Afghan and **Saluki**

Dandie dinmont

Maltese

Irish Water Spaniel

Finnish Hound has ears described as 'ailerons'

Blushers

Pharaoh hounds (their ears go pink with excitement!)

Wrinklies

Basenji

Basset

Bloodhound

Bulldog

Bull mastiff

Black and tan coonhound

Chow

Mastiff (when excited)

Pekingese

Shar-pei

Tosa

Ugly Mugs (some say)

Boxer

Bulldog

Bull terrier

Brussels griffon

Shar-pei

Foot Note

Hairy Feet

Afghan hound

Clumber spaniel
Ibizan hound
Irish setter
Lhasa apso

Papillon.

Papillon
Pekingese
Saluki
Samoyed
Tibetan terrier

Odd Feet

Pyrenean mountain dog
(double dew claw)
Lundehound (extra toe)
Akita (webbed feet)
Leonberger (webbed feet)
Newfoundland (webbed feet)
Weimeraner (webbed feet)

Leg Lines

Bandy Legs

Basset
Bulldog
Dachshund
Dandie dinmont
Mexican hairless
Pekingese

Funny Walks

Bloodhound
Irish water spaniel (sailor's roll)
Otterhound
Pekingese (waddle)
Sussex spaniel (characteristic swing)

The Tail End

Born Bobtails (sometimes)

Brittany spaniel
Chihuahua (rarely)
Dobermann pinscher (originally)
Old English sheepdog
Puli
Lapland spitz
Welsh Pembroke corgi
Valee sheepdog

Prize Waggers

Cocker spaniel
Munsterlander (constant)
Old English sheepdog (wags whole body)
Pharaoh hound

The Bone Crushers

Boxer
Bulldog
Bull terrier
Drever
Eskimo dog
Fila Brasileira
Komondor
Maremma
Mastiffs
Mountain dogs

Rubery Bull Terrier.

Rottweiler

Terriers

Biters and Fighters

*The dog, to gain some private
ends,
Went mad and bit the man . . .
The man recover'd of his bite,
The dog it was that died.*

Oliver Goldsmith
Elegy on the Death of a Mad Dog

Decisive Biters

A **Chesapeake Bay retriever** in 1840 bit the footman of a rich widow, thus ending his owner's hopes of marrying money. The owner, John Trevanion of Caerhays Castle, commissioned a huge painting of the dog shortly before the family finally went broke.

A police dog attacked Janus Gundlaugsson just before a football match between his team, Fortuna Cologne, and another German second division team. Fortuna lost the match and appealed for a replay because the bite had been so severe that Gundlaugsson could not play. The appeal was rejected.

They say that if a dog bites a man, it's a story; and if a man bites a dog it's a good story. Well, RIN TIN TIN was a one-man dog and was quite capable of biting his co-starring actors as soon as the cameras stopped rolling. Charles Hargan often did fight scenes with the dog and after a typical rough-and-tumble Rinty suddenly bit him on his padded leg. Hargan bit him back, on the ear, and the dog never nipped him again.

A certain doctor used to carry a small snuff box with him when out shooting. Why? 'Dogfights. Dog can't sneeze and bite.'

Dogfighters

Boston terrier

Bull terrier

Shar-pei

Staffordshire terrier

Staffordshire bull terrier

Tosa

Quarrelers

Alaskan malamute

Fox terrier

Glen of Imaal terrier

Ibizan hound

Canaan dog

Affenpinscher

Unfriendly dogs

Fila brasileira (judges cannot touch them)

Japanese spaniel (peevish)

Spitz varieties (suspicious of strangers)

Tibetan mastiff (ferocious when trained to be).

Eating Habits

*I'm a lean dog, a keen dog, a
wild dog, and alone.*

Irene Rutherford McLeod
Lone Dog

Greedy

Belgian sheepdog

Cocker spaniel

English setter

Labrador retriever

Frugal

Italian hound

Kyushu

Pyrenean mastiff

Fish-eaters

Eskimo dog

Iceland dog

Lapphund.

The Senses

A Good Nose

All sorts of theories have been put
forward about the best dogs for
scenting. It was said, for example,
that a dish-faced pointer was
preferable because the nose was
higher and could therefore smell
better. Hounds are the top noses
and, like most other dogs, they
can probably detect fear, anger
and exhaustion in the scent of
their prey. Bloodhounds are
supreme, and in 1688 they used to
rub a bloodhound's nose in
vinegar to quicken his scent.

The greater the olefactory cell
area, the greater the sense of
smell. An average man has four
square centimetres of such cells, a
German shepherd 200, a basset
125 and a fox terrier 150.

Bloodhound (top tracker,
interested only in the trail)

Otterhound (as good as a
bloodhound, including in water)

Fila brasileiro (good in rivers
and swamps)

Norwegian elkhound (can smell
elk from several kilometres)

Hounds of all kinds (e.g. basset,
foxhound, buhund)

Pointers and **Setters**

Labradors and **Retrievers**

Vizsla

Alaskan malamute

Truffle dogs (bassets, terriers
and mongrels)

Cavalier King Charles

Excellent Hearing

Airedale

Briard

Lhasa apso

Pharaoh hound

Poodle

Saluki

Excellent Eyesight

Buhund

Collie

Greyhound

King Charles spaniel

Sense of Direction and Homing Instinct

American foxhound (superb)

Alaskan malamute

Briquet

Pharaoh hound

Poodle

Most hunting hounds.

Leetbank Pharaoh Hounds.

Very Clean Dogs

Apart from keeping themselves particularly clean, often in the same way as a cat does, many of these dogs have little or no 'doggy' smell:

Akita

Alaskan malamute

Basenji

Chinese crested dog

Dalmatian

Keeshond

Kyushu

Pug

Saluki

Standard schnauzer

Stinker

Otterhound (because of his oily waterproof coat).

Longevity

In general, the bigger the dog the shorter its lifespan. A good average age for an Irish wolfhound would be 8–10 years, and for a toy dog 18–20 years (though very small toys tend to be short lived). Spitz types and fox terriers often reach 18 or 20, but boxers and German shepherd dogs can be old at 12 or 13, with boxers often not reaching 10. Dobermann pinschers, however, can live to 15 or even 20, and shih-tzus easily make 15.

Dalmatian.

In 1900 the average lifespan for all breeds of dog was only seven. Today it is 11 or 12, thanks to improved veterinary facilities and better feeding.

ADJUTANT was a labrador retriever who died aged 27.

POODLES of three generations were recorded by the American Kennel Club as reaching at least the age of 20.

JUDY was a Tibetan temple dog who died in Petworth, Sussex, aged 22. Her owner's previous dog, RUSTY, had died at 19. The cats had long lives too!

Barking

Let dogs delight to bark and bite,
For God hath made them so.

Isaac Watts
Divine Songs For Children Against
Quarrelling

Non-Barkers (can't or don't)

Wolves, jackals, dingos and Eskimo dogs never bark—they howl. Some domesticated dogs cannot bark either and will howl, yodel or chortle instead. Other dogs rarely bark.

Akita (seldom)

Alaskan malamute

Australian shepherd dog (half bark, half howl if necessary)

Basenji (chortles and yodels)

Borzoi

Chinese crested dog (never noisy)

Clumber spaniel (mute hunter)

Dingo (no bark but its voice carries well)

Eskimo dog (howler)

Kyushu

Pyrenean mastiff

Telomian (polite bark or happy yodel)

Affenpinscher.

Barkers

Terriers and bored dogs bark the most and the loudest, but it is unfair to say that 'cowardly dogs bark loudest' (John Webster). Terriers are famous for their courage and impudence! Apart from the terriers, the barkers include:

Affenpinscher

Appenzell mountain dog

Brussels griffon (irrepressible)

Dachshund

Finnish spitz

Hovawart (strong and sonorous)

Little lion dog (intense)

Lapponian herder

Mexican hairless dog

Miniature schnauzer

Old English sheepdog (loud with a 'pot cassee' ring to it)

Pinscher

Samoyed (frequent and lively)

Sussex spaniel (continuously when working)

Tibetan terrier (very unusual: starts deep and rises like a siren)

Noisy Dogs

Pug (snort, snore, snuffle and grunt)

Pharaoh (very loud yawn indeed)

Musical Voices

All the hounds 'sing'. George Washington described his foxhounds as 'like the bells of Moscow'. The voices of American foxhounds have been used in pop songs.

Talkers

Sussex spaniels talk to themselves constantly while hunting, and their owners can tell by their voices what kind of game they are following. Poodles are reckoned to be the most able to understand the spoken word.

AND NOW THE NEWS...

Character

Cob was the strongest, Mob was the wrongest,
Chittaboob's tail was the finest and longest.

Rev. Richard Harris Barham
The Ingoldsby Legends: The Truants

Good-natured and Kind

Afghan hound

Basset hound

Briard

Bernese mountain dog

Bloodhound

Borzoi

Bouvier des Flandres

Bulldog (despite appearances and history)

Cocker spaniel

English springer spaniel

Great Dane.

Great Dane

Irish terrier

Irish wolfhound (one of the gentlest breeds of all)

Kuvasz

Little lion dog

Newfoundland

Poodle

St Bernard

Skye terrier

Spinone (no one has ever been bitten by one)

Slow and Steady (or even lazy)

Basset hound (slow reflexes)

Clumber spaniel (ideal for similarly overweight sportsmen)

Wire-haired pointing griffon (designed for the older sportsman on foot)

Deerhound (when not chasing)

Harlequin Great Dane (phlegmatic)

Serious

Bolognese (very)
Bull mastiff
Clumber spaniel
Italian pointer
Portuguese water dog
Samoyed

Polite

Bloodhound
Brittany spaniel
Bull terrier

Chow Chow.

Chow
Clumber spaniel
Gordon setter
Skye terrier

Possessive and Protective

Catahoula leopard dog
Fox terrier
German wire-haired pointer
Norwich terrier (very protective of its puppies)
Puli
Portuguese water dog

Rottweiler
Rough collie
Spitz (various)
Most sheepdogs

Independent

The dog will come when he is called,
The cat will turn away;
The Pekingese will please itself
Whatever you may say.

E. V. Lucas
The More I See Of Men...

Bergamasco (stubborn)
Bichon frise (strong temperament)
Borzoi (reserved and sometimes stubborn)
Brussels griffon (disobedient)
Chinese Imperial Ch'in (a most demanding dog)
Chow (will die for its master but not obey him)
Dalmatian
Eskimo dog (intractable)
Greyhound (reserved)
Irish setter
Kerry blue (stubborn)
Lakeland terrier (stubborn)
Pekingese
Poodle (character)
Rough collie
Siberian husky (very stubborn)
Weimeraner
Welsh springer spaniel

Sensitive

Afghan hound (needs to be trained kindly)
Aidi (very nervous)
Airedale (needs to feel loved and respected)

Bloodhound (a pleasantly shy dog)

Brittany spaniel (timid if treated roughly)

Chinese Imperial Ch'in (the most sensitive of dogs)

Cocker spaniel (gentle training)

Dalmatian (needs humans or becomes melancholy)

Deerhound (shy, but one of the best of man's companions)

Eskimo dog (diffident if harshly treated)

Italian greyhound (timid)

King Charles spaniel (timid)

Maltese (easily alarmed by suspicious noises)

Poodle (can read your mind)

Scottish terrier (sensitive to criticism and praise)

Incurably Curious

Affenpinscher

Aidi

Brussels griffon

Pharaoh hound

Schipperke

Toy fox terrier

Dogged Dogs

It's dogged as does it. It ain't thinking about it.

Trollope
Last Chronicle of Barset

American Fox Hound (8–12 hours trail-running)

Brazilian Tracker (6–7 hours tracking jaguar)

Coonhounds (never give up and go through any terrain)

Dachshund (slow, steady and sure)

English Fox Hound (15–20 miles to the meet, 50 miles running)

Dachshunds.

73

Gordon Setter (can work longer than most without a drink)

Harrier (prey sometimes collapses of exhaustion)

Karelian Bear Dog (very stubborn, lone hunter)

Sled Dogs (Alaskan malamutes, Eskimo dogs etc.–constant running for many miles and many hours heavily laden)

Welsh Springer Spaniel (tireless hunter).

Borzoi.

Agile Dogs

Afghan Hound–twists and turns, and can leap like a monkey

Ibizan Hound–can jump high from a standstill

Old English Sheepdog–very agile at speed

Pharaoh Hound–very lithe and agile

Pointer–athletic.

Fast Dogs

Greyhound takes the prize most of the time. It is the 18th fastest land mammal in the world, reaching 43 mph (70 kilometres per hour). Among dogs, it is the fastest breed in the world for distances up to half a mile, after which it can be passed by a **Whippet**. The top speed is of course the peak speed in a sprint and cannot be maintained for long, but an average of 41.72 mph (66.7 km/hour) has been recorded over 410 yards (375 metres). Some popular winners from the past are:

CHIEF PILOT covered 650 yards (594 metres) at a rate of 38 mph in Australia, maintaining a speed of 38.5 mph over the first 440 yards (402 metres).

MASTER MAGRATH celebrated courser owned by Lord Lurgan, raced from 1867 to 1873, was beaten only once, won the Waterloo Cup three years in succession.

MICK THE MILLER Born in 1926, winner of the Derby twice then won 19 consecutive races.

PIGALLE WONDER 525 yards (480 metres) in 28.4 seconds in Derby heats, and he also broke 29 seconds and many records.

TREV'S PERFECTION won the English Greyhound Derby in 28.95 seconds over a distance of 525 yards, averaging 37.1 mph.

Whippet–better than a greyhound at maintaining speed if the distance is more than half a mile, but was bred for snap trials where its remarkable acceleration was fully tested. A time of 12 seconds over 200 yards (183 metres) is not unusual (a trained human athlete might do 100 yards (91 metres) in 10 seconds and a very fast racehorse's speed over one and a half miles would be a fraction of a second slower than the sprinting whippet's). A speed of 35.5 mph (56.8 km/hour) over

200 yards (183 metres) has been recorded for a whippet.

Saluki—slightly faster than the **Afghan**: 43 mph has been claimed, and one was said to have been paced by a car travelling at 55 mph. However, such feats are not as carefully monitored and timed as greyhound speeds.

Borzoi—some say they can be faster than greyhounds when coursing jackals.

Hunt-Addicts

Like a dog, he hunts in dreams.
Tennyson
Locksley Hall

Beagle
Border Terrier
Coonhound
Pharaoh Hound
Pointer

And just about every breed of hound and spaniel there is.

Ch. Kaplar's Kwik Step to Sundust, American Spaniel.

Wanderers

Any full-blooded male dog will wander if bitches are on heat but some breeds tend to go off on their own anyway whenever they can, particularly the following:

Beagle
Bolognese
Puli
Pumi
Setters
Spaniels (Welsh Springer the worst).

Very Trainable (intelligent) Dogs

Most sheepdog breeds are highly intelligent and easy to train to their work—and usually *need* to work. Gun dogs are also very responsive to training, as are some of the closer cousins of wild dogs. One or two of the smaller breeds are exceptionally good at performing tricks. Here are some very good learners:

Aidi
American Water Spaniel
Anatolian Shepherd Dog
Brittany Spaniel
Cairn Terrier (tricks)
Canaan Dog
Catalan Sheepdog
Collie (particularly the Border and Smooth breeds)
Corgi
German Shepherd Dog (which *must* work)
Huntaway
Kelpie
Poodle (tricks)

Golden Retriever dog and cross puppy.

Retrievers (labrador, golden, flat-coated)

Rottweiler

Schipperke.

Dogs with Long Memories

Belgian sheepdog

Bergamasco

Dalmatian

Valee sheepdog.

Down-and-Stay

In the summer of 1985 there was a sponsored Down Stay in aid of Hearing Dogs for the Deaf at Haslemere in Surrey. The dogs were all members of a first-time training class, and eight out of twelve managed to 'down and stay' for the full 15 minutes in spite of the rain:

SHEBA, collie (8 months old, only four lessons)

POLLY, cavalier King Charles spaniel (2½ years old)

CINDY, cavalier King Charles spaniel (1 year old)

EMMA, mongrel (15 months old)

HUGO, Airedale (3 years old)-

TANDY, sheltie (3 years old)

KELLY, collie (8 months old)

SHENA, collie (to become a collector for Guide Dogs for the Blind when she is older)

The youngest dog in the group, BRUCE (golden retriever aged 5½ months) managed seven minutes.

Snow Dogs

A traveller, by the faithful hound,
Half-buried in the snow was found.

Longfellow
Excelsior

The main northern snow dogs include four pure Arctic breeds:

Alaskan Malamute

Eskimo Dog

Samoyed

Siberian Husky

There are many other snow dogs, particularly in Scandinavia. Here are some of them:

Haldenstover

Iceland Dog

Norwegian Elkhound

St Bernard

Schillerstovare

The main work of snow dogs includes hauling sledges, hunting and rescue work. Even collies and setters have been used in sledge racing, which is now a family sport but which also remains serious work in some parts. Here are some sledge facts:

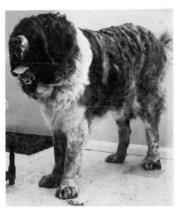

Shandy, St Bernard.

Eskimo Dogs In the 19th century a four-dog team would draw loads of up to 400 lbs (181.4 kg) for more than 30 miles (48 km) a day. A team of seven would draw a sledgeful of men a mile (1.7 km) in four and a half minutes, and one Captain Lyons said that three dogs drew him the same distance in six minutes on a laden sledge weighing a 100 lbs (45.3 kg). His dogs were capable of galloping at full speed on a pitch-dark night through blowing snow without putting a foot wrong and always straight towards his destination. They were a quarrelsome crew, snapping and snarling at each other as they galloped and sometimes tumbling into a general fight and chaos. The Eskimos rarely fed the dogs properly: they existed on scraps of hide, fish and seal bones, and Captain Hall once witnessed a single dog eating a piece of walrus hide and blubber six feet (1.82 m) long in seven seconds. Some teams could eat nothing for 48 hours and still travel 70 miles (112.7 km), returning home fresh and perky.

Stories about Eskimo dogs and their strength, speed and perseverance are legion. For example:

MACMILLAN continuous 100 mile (160 km) run in less than 18 hours.

KANE six-dog team with 700 lb load, 750 miles (1,207 km) in two weeks.

Sledge-racing is a family sport which even eight-year-old children can enter (with one dog). Some race times (for sport and for real) are:

20 teams in relays, 675 miles (1,086 km) in 127.5 hours (to carry vital diphtheria antitoxin to Nome, Alaska)

Dr Roland Lombard, a vet from Massachusetts, won the Anchorage world championship for the sixth time in 1970: 75 miles (120 km) in 324 minutes.

SNOWBIRD, a famous malamute, in 1910 was the lead dog in a team which pulled half a ton 1,100 miles (1,770 km) over a mountain range. A fortnight later he led the victorious team in the First All-Alaska Sweepstakes, covering 408 miles (656 km) in just over 72 hours.

Shipwrecked Dogs

At least three breeds are claimed to have owed their creation to shipwrecks:

Chesapeake Bay Retriever In 1807 an English ship was wrecked off Maryland and two Newfoundland puppies were rescued, one red and one black. They were eventually mated with local retrievers, water dogs or coonhounds, and the new breed became a superb water dog, working in rough seas and protected by its coarse, oily coat. The Chesapeake is a very independent, courageous and determined dog.

Kerry Blue Terrier

Apart from a claim that the Kerry blue was in Noah's Ark, it is also claimed that the only survivor of a shipwreck off the Kerry coast was a very fierce terrier which killed every dog it met and thus established the right to found its own breed.

Skye Terrier

In 1588 the Spanish Armada lost most of its ships off the west coast of Scotland. It is said that some white Spanish dogs from the wrecks landed on the Isle of Skye, and Lady Macdonald of Armadale Castle crossed them with local dogs to create the Skye terrier. Like other animals on the Scottish isles, Skyes grew coats well adapted to the climate: their double coat consists of a very long outer coat insulated with an inner one of short wool.

Labrador Retrievers

Not so much shipwrecked as shipped, labradors first came to England by boat, landing at Poole in the 1830s. They had long been used as fishermen's dogs in Labrador.

Kiskas Bulletproof, Red Akita.

Labradors and retrievers
Leonberger
Newfoundland
Otterhound
Picardy spaniel
Poodle
Portuguese water dog
Pudelpointer
Puli
Schipperke
Setters
Vizsla
Water spaniels
Welsh springer spaniel

Water Dogs

Akita
Barbet
Brittany spaniel
Griffon nivernais
Irish terrier
Keeshond
Kyushu

Big Game Hunters

Dogs have been used as hunting aids from earliest times: it was a natural expression of the instincts and symbiotic relationship of man and dog. All over the world dogs were trained to find, flush, pursue or attack different prey. For example, the Patagonians hunted herds of guanacos with the aid of horses and dogs: the dogs were trained to seize the prey. Gran Chaco dogs, which were fed on offal and scraps and lived in dens which they scraped in the ground, were essential for hunting jaguar and peccary: they were noisy and persistent little curs which so aggravated the fleeing jaguar that it paused to deal with them, giving the hunter an opportunity to catch up! Eskimo dogs, apart from drawing sledges, were trained to detect seals' breathing holes in the ice, and also to attack a bear from the rear so that the hunter could harpoon it. In Tierra del Fuego fox-like dogs herded shoals of fish into nets and stole edible birds' nests for their masters. In Samoa they trained very courageous and skilful dogs to check the progress of a fleeing pig by catching it by the ears, shoulders and tail so that the hunter could finish it off. The Kaffirs knew that elephants dreaded small animals, especially dogs, which they used to divert a charge. Here are some more specialist big-game hunters:

Afghan wolf, gazelle, leopard, jackal, fox

Airedale bear, wolf, wild boar, stag, otter

Akita bear, deer

Beagle (oversize ones in Ceylon and Venezuela) jaguar, leopard

Borzoi wolf coursing and throwing

Brazilian Tracker jaguar tracking

Bull Mastiff poachers (trained to throw down but not maul)

Coonhounds raccoon, stag, bear, opossum, cougar, wildcat

Coursing Hounds coyote (American Great Plains)

Finnish Spitz polar bear, elk

Great Dane wild boar

Greyhound stag, gazelle, wild boar, fox, hare (not to mention domestic cats and geese!)

Harrier leopards (Ceylon), large cats (South America)

Hokkaidoken bear (Japan)

Irish Wolfhound stag, wolf, coyote, wild boar

Kangaroo Hound kangaroo

Karelian Bear Dog bear, elk

Norwegian Elkhound elk

Plott Hound stag, coyote, wolf, wildcat

Pomeranian polar bear (before the breed was bantamised)

Mastiff.

Rhodesian Ridgeback lion

Saluki gazelle (with falcons), jackal (US)

Scottish Deerhound deer

Swedish Elkhound elk, bear.

The Specialists

Most dogs have been bred or developed for special purposes. Here are some of the more unusual specialities:

Bulldogs and similar breeds were used to bait bulls—not merely for spectator sport but also because butchers believed that the practice tenderised the beef.

Chinese Imperial Ch'in is a dog that spent most of its day in meditation. It used to be very much a court dog: in one ancient Chinese court about a hundred of the dogs would stand up on their hindlegs at the entrance of the Empress and would remain upright until she was seated.

Coonhounds were bred in America specifically as raccoon hunters but they are also used for bear, opossum, cougar, stag, fox and wildcat. The 'treeing' breeds literally clamber into trees in pursuit of their prey. The dogs now take part in rough and tough trials, by day and by night, which involve swimming in fast streams and climbing trees.

Eastern Greyhounds (e.g. Afghan and borzoi) were trained to hunt as a brace. The bitch attacked the prey's hindquarters, attempting to hamstring it, and the dog went for the throat. Borzois were supposed to pin a wolf rather than kill it.

Elk Hounds were bred for the pursuit of elk and bear. They have special hunting methods: they slither over the snow, cut off the prey's line of retreat and drive it into gun range.

Fila Brasileiro hounds were originally trained to kill Indians in battle and later to capture runaway slaves.

Heeler is a type of cattle dog which bites the heels of its charges and quickly drops flat to avoid being kicked.

Ch. Gavimir Nighthawk, Keeshond.

Keeshond is a dog-of-all-trades on Dutch boats.

Kelpies are superb Australian sheepdogs which can do the work of six men and cover more than forty miles a day. They separate the sheep for drinking at the water-hole, and have perfected the art of walking (and running) on the backs of enclosed sheep. They also practise the unique skill of Tinning the Chicken, when they herd a chick into a tin can.

Labrador Retrievers were originally fishermen's dogs. Their main task was to swim to and from the boats dragging nets and ropes.

Lundehund is a breed specifically trained to retrieve puffins' nests, which are edible. The dog climbs a cliff, puts the bird to flight, grabs the nest and brings it to its master. If it is working in caves it can close its ears to keep out dripping water.

Nova Scotia Duck-tolling Dogs have one function: to excite the curiosity of wildfowl by creating a disturbance on the shore. In theory the ducks are so intrigued that they come and investigate, and the wildfowler then takes aim. (The natural reaction of wildfowl to any predator–e.g. a fox on the shore–is to swim towards it en masse: thus every bird is aware of the predator, which cannot hope to make a sneak attack and often slinks away in disgust with a fleet of ducks shadowing its progress along the bank.)

Portuguese Water Dogs, like labrador retrievers, were fishermen's dogs for centuries. As well as catching ropes, they also brought back fish which had escaped from the nets.

Tibetan spaniel.

Shar-peis are probably the oddest-looking dogs we know today. They were developed for dog fights, and their excessively loose and wrinkled skin, with its pig-like bristles, and their very small ears, did not give opponents much to grip.

Tibetan Spaniels were originally used to turn prayer wheels, act as sentinels, and be hot-water bottles for their owners.

Tosa Mastiffs are a Japanese breed originally developed for ceremonial dog-fights. They were paraded during festivals dressed up in silk and gold blankets and controlled on the end of huge thick ropes.

Whippets have been called the most perfect racing machine ever fashioned by man. They were bred by miners in northern England for snap trials, the aim of which was to achieve the quickest kill of a rabbit in an enclosed area.

Rare Breeds

Some breeds are very common locally but rarely seen elsewhere. Some are only described as rare because they are difficult to classify as being different from another established breed, or

Portuguese Water Dog.

because they are the same breed by a different name. Many breeds have been close to extinction but have been rescued by enthusiastic breeders; others have at some time been lost but have been 'recreated'. A rare breed today may be quite a popular one tomorrow, and vice versa–breeds are very susceptible to the whims of fashion. There are approximately 850 different breeds in the world, many of them obscure and local, and only 116 are recognised by the American Kennel Club and 147 in the English Kennel Club regulations (of which about 60 are native British breeds, and most of them on the books for more than a century). This list gives some of the rare breeds by various definitions:

Barbet a famous water breed and pointer which looks like a typical shaggy sheepdog, said to be the father of all pointers and of the poodle

Beauceron a French sheepdog, similar to a Dobermann

Bleu de Gascon French hounds of two varieties

Chinook is a rare breed originally developed in the USA as a sled dog. There is now a total of 76, all in the USA.

Clumber Spaniel solid, old-fashioned, thoughtful dog for the stouter sportsman; very rare outside Britain

Drever Swedish trailing hound

Field Spaniel the rarest of the British spaniels

Fila Brasileiro close to extinction in the 1940s, saved when all Brazilian embassies began to have one

Glen of Imaal Terrier.

Glen of Imaal Terrier tough old Irish breed from County Wicklow, not recognised by the English Kennel Club until 1975

Chinook.

Ch. Marianne of Raycroft.

Giant Schnauzer saved from extinction in 1914 and 1950

Iceland Dog close to extinction in the 16th century and again early this century

Irish Water Spaniel ancient type of puce-coloured curly-coated dog similar to the Portuguese water dog; now very low numbers in Britain and USA

Kangaroo Hound cross between greyhound and Irish wolfhound developed in Australia in the 1850s for coursing kangaroo; now quite rare

Giant Schnauzer.

Little Lion Dog.

Little Lion Dog (Löwchen) breed probably several centuries old but never very popular; clipped to emphasise its 'lion look'

Nova Scotia Duck-tolling Dog plume-tailed fox-red breed developed as a duck decoy from Chesapeake Bay retriever

Old English Mastiff only 35 registered in this country in 1908, only three litters born during World War II, only 20 animals left in the UK in 1945 and mostly too old for breeding, but stock was imported from the USA and the breed was saved

Portuguese East African Hunting Dog

Pudelpointer

Puffinhound or Lundehund

Sinhala Hound the native dog of Ceylon

Soft-coated Wheaten Terrier sensible, shaggy, freedom-loving, all-purpose Irish terrier, nearly extinct as pure breed in 1930s but rescued by Dr Gerard J. Pierse and others; now more popular in USA than UK

Sussex Spaniel very rare, even in England—only ten registered in UK in 1947 and only four in USA in 1970

Tibetan Mastiff ferocious fighter, claimed by Aristotle to be a cross between dog and tiger, and described by Marco Polo as being as big as an ass

Tosa Dog Japanese ceremonial fighting dog

Vallhund.

Look-alikes

Cats is 'dogs', rabbits is 'dogs', and so's Parrats.

Punch
Vol 1 vi (1869)

Crocodile
Field spaniel (a less-than-polite 19th-century description—it was also called a caterpillar)

Dachshund (Konrad Lorenz called his Kroki)

Lion

Bichon (various)

Chow

Foo dog (imaginary Buddhist lion dog)

Lhasa apso (claimed to be the true lion dog of Tibet)

Lowchen (the name means 'little lion')

Pekingese

Poodle (in classic 'lion' trim)

Rhodesian ridgeback (originally called the Rhodesian ridgeback lion dog because it hunted lions)

Shih-tzu ('lion head, bear torso, camel hoof, feather duster tail, palm-leaf ears, nice teeth, pearly petal tongue, and movement like a goldfish' is the original required standard!)

Monkey

Affenpinscher

Cao da Serra de Aires

Pug

Pig/Hog

Mexican hairless dog (the pups look like naked pink piglets, and the dogs have pig-like teeth)

Shar-pei (pig-like coat)

Shar-pei.

Sheep

Bedlington terrier

Bergamasco and **Valee sheepdog**

Komondor (very much a 'wolf in sheep's clothing')

Puli (black sheep!)

and many other European shepherd dogs like **briard**, **Pyrenees sheepdog**, **Catalan sheepdog** and, with imagination, **Old English sheepdog** and **bearded collie**.

Wolf

Alaskan malamute (said to be a dog/wolf cross or a tame wolf: it was claimed that bitches were

tied to a tree outside camp so that they could mate with wolves)

German shepherd dog (called Alsatian wolfdog in post-war Britain).

Motherhood

Litter sizes range from one to about 15 or 16 and on average the larger the breed the larger the litter. In most breeds the bitches come into season twice a year, but the basenji only has one heat a year, like most wild dogs. Sometimes record litters are produced though it is rare for all the pups to survive.

Big Litters

American Foxhound called LENA claimed to have whelped 23 puppies in June 1944, but they were not registered and could have been two or even three litters.

St Bernard whelped 23, but 11 died while the application for registration was being made.

Great Dane largest litter registered by AKC is 19, though in one case there is a claim for 21.

Bloodhound 17 in one litter in 1917, all survived. On average, bloodhounds have 9–16 in a litter,

and there is a claim for 19 in the last century.

Irish Setter 18, 16 and 15 in successive years to the same bitch.

Dobermann Pinscher 17 is the AKC record for the breed.

Other Breeds

16 Chesapeake Bay retriever, collie, English setter, English springer spaniel, German shepherd dog, German short-haired and wire-haired pointer, golden retriever, Newfoundland, weimeraner.
15 Airedale, boxer, bouvier des Flandres, Brittany spaniel, Dalmatian, Irish water spaniel, labrador retriever, poodle.

Problem Mothers

Boston Terrier usually needs Caesarean

Brussels Griffon irregular season, does not always conceive, small litter (often one pup) prone to postnatal deaths

Bulldog often infertile; usually need Caesarean if they do give birth, and then they are such hopeless mothers that fosters must be found

Irish Setter Emma with 15 of her 18 pups born March 1981.

Briard puppies.

Eskimo Dog sometimes eat the pups if they are not left alone (natural instinct of many wild animals)

Finnish Spitz pups are very delicate

Japanese Spaniel very difficult to rear the pups, even if they are born alive

Mastiff accident-prone—the mother often manages to lie on the pups and squash them to death

Pomeranian puppies.

Pomeranian pups very delicate and small (you can hold three in the palm of your hand)

Yorkshire Terrier usually needs veterinary supervision when whelping.

Odd Fosters

In Paraguay and Peru dogs were so highly esteemed that human wet-nurses looked after orphan pups.

In England in the early 18th century, spaniel bitches were used to foster 'sow babbies' to sweeten the pork so that it would 'eat as fine as any Puppy Dog'.

The father of the well-known Victorian painter, Landseer, had a bitch which fostered a lion cub in 1820. Orphan tiger cubs have been known to be fostered on bitches too.

A Newfoundland living in Sussex recently adopted a duckling: they became inseparable. There was also a hen which brooded some orphan pups.

Cultured Dogs

Training a man takes time. Some men are a little slow to respond, but a dog who makes allowances and tries to put himself in the man's place will be rewarded with a loyal pal. Men are apt to be highly strung and sensitive, and a dog who loses his temper will only break the man's spirit. Not every dog who tries to bring up a man is successful.

Corey Ford
Every Dog Should Own a Man

Literary Dogs

BASKET Gertrude Stein's white poodle

BEAU William Cowper's spaniel in *The Dog and the Water Lily*

BLEMIE Eugene O'Neill's dalmatian

BOATSWAIN Lord Byron's Newfoundland

BOUNCE Alexander Pope's Great Dane

BROWNIE T. H. White's Irish setter

CHARLEY John Steinbeck's large poodle

CHOUGNA Victor Hugo's 'very exasperating dog'

COLL Chaucer–'Coll, our dog'

DAISY E. B. White's Scottish terrier

DART William Wordsworth's greyhound

DASH Charles Lamb's big unruly dog, gift from Thomas Hood

FLUSH Elizabeth Barrett Browning's spaniel

FOP William Cowper's spaniel

GEIST, MAX and KAISER Matthew Arnold's dachshunds (Kaiser was part collie)

JO-FI Sigmund Freud's chow

LUATH J. M. Barrie's Newfoundland, model for Nana

MONSIEUR GRAT Rene Descartes' dog

MUSIC William Wordsworth's greyhound

NERO Thomas Carlyle's wife's Maltese cross

PELLEAS Maurice Maeterlinck's French bulldog

PRITCHARD Alexandre Dumas' pointer (a thief)

WESSEX Thomas Hardy's wire-haired fox terrier.

The Bronte Dogs

FLOSSY (Anne's small spaniel)

KEEPER (Emily's ugly, uncontrollable and devoted bull mastiff)

Robert Burns' Twa Dogs, who 'rejoiced they were na men':

CAESAR (the rich man's pet)

LUATH (the ploughman's collie)

Charles Dickens

BULL'S-EYE (Bill Sikes's bull terrier in *Oliver Twist*)

DIOGENES (gruff and scruffy dog in *Dombey and Son*)

Flossy, *watercolour by Charlotte Bronte*

Keeper, *watercolour by Emily Bronte.*

Oliver Reed as Sikes with Bull's Eye from Oliver.

JIP (Dora Spenlow's little black spaniel in *David Copperfield*)

MERRYLEGS (juggler Jupes's performing dog in *Hard Times*)

PONTO (Mr Jingles' pointer in *The Pickwick Papers*)

TIMBER DOODLE (little white spaniel given to Dickens and renamed SNITTLE TIMBERY)

Sir Arthur Conan Doyle

CARLO (vicious mastiff in *The Adventure of the Copper Beeches*; also a spaniel in *The Adventure of the Sussex Vampire*)

THE HOUND OF THE BASKERVILLES (ghostly black beast of Dartmoor)

Rudyard Kipling

BOOTS and SLIPPERS (Aberdeen terrier narrators in *Thy Servant a Dog*)

GARM (bull terrier)

RAVAGER (old one-eyed hound, friend of Boots and Slippers)

TEEM (little French truffle dog in *Teem, A Treasure-Hunter*)

Konrad Lorenz

HIRSCHMANN (Hanover schweisshund)

PYGI (aloof, independent chow bitch belonging to Lorenz's wife)

STASI (exceptionally faithful cross-breed in *Man Meets Dog*)

TITO (alsatian bitch, so attuned to her master's feelings that she would nip the backside of anyone who was irritating him)

WOLF (chow)

Beatrix Potter

DUCHESS (little black dog in *The Pie and the Patty Pan*)

JOHN JOINER (terrier in *The Roly-Poly Pudding*)

PICKLES (terrier in *Ginger & Pickles*)

STUMPY (large brown dog in *The Tale of Little Pig Robinson*)

TIPKINS (little dog in the Stumpy story)

Sir Walter Scott

BEVIS (mastiff in *Woodstock*)

LUFRA (Douglas's fleet hound in *The Lady of the Lake*)

MAIDA (a cross between 'the deer grey-hound and the mastiff with a shaggy mane like a lion', Scott's favourite dog, big as a Shetland pony and terrified of the cat; one of the most painted dogs ever)

Sir Walter Scott *by William Nicholson.*

MUSTARD and PEPPER (auld, young and little–Dandie Dinmont's terriers in *Guy Mannering*)

ROSWAL (majestic hound in *The Talisman*)

Shakespeare

CRAB (the only dog which actually appears in a Shakespearean play, in *The Two Gentlemen of Verona*)

LADY (brach or hound mentioned in *Henry IV*, part I)

THESEUS' HOUNDS (*A Midsummer Night's Dream*)

TRAY, BLANCHE and SWEETHEART (mentioned in *King Lear* and described by the mad king as 'little dogs')

James Thurber

BARGE (who became addicted to alcohol and killed himself in shame)

MUGGS (Airedale, *The Dog That Bit People*, but terrified of thunder)

And a host of other Thurber dogs, including JOSEPHINE, DARIEN, FEELY, JEANNIE, CRISTABEL.

The list of dogs in literature is almost an endless one. Here is a mixed bag of fictional characters, some based on real dogs.

ALIDORO mastiff, *Pinocchio*

ATHOS *Ulysses*

BOB wire-haired terrier, *Poirot Loses a Client*

BONES mongrel, *A Yellow Dog*

BOSY bouvier des Flandres, *The World of Bemelmans*

BOWSER THE HOUND in Thornton Burgess nature books

BUCK St Bernard/Scotch shepherd, *The Call of the Wild*

BUGLE ANN foxhound, *The Voice of Bugle Ann*

CIPION and BERGANZA *Colloquy of the Dogs*, 1613

DANDY lazy shaggy mongrel, *Ludlam's Dog*

DOUGAL mastiff, *Little Lord Fauntleroy*

DUKE mongrel, *Penrod*

FIDELE and MEDJI *Diary of a Madman*

GAMIN poodle, *Gentle Julia*

GARRYOWEN red mongrel, *Ulysses*

GENEVIEVE hound, *Madeline's Rescue*

GISSING talking dog, *Where the Blue Begins*

HARRY white with black spots, *Harry the Dirty Dog*

JENNIE sealyham, *Higglety Pigglety Pop!*

JIP '*The Story of Doctor Dolittle*'

JOSEPHINE poodle, *Every Night, Josephine!*

KASHTANKA red mongrel, *Kashtanka*

LAD collie, *Lad: A Dog*

LUATH labrador and BODGER bull terrier *The Incredible Journey*

McINTOSH Aberdeen terrier, *Jeeves and the Dog McIntosh*

MEPHISTOPHELES poodle, *Faust*

MUNDO CANI DOG noisy hound, *The Book of the Dun Cow*

MUTT mongrel, *The Dog Who Wouldn't Be*

NOX black retriever, *The Incredulity of Father Brown*

OWD BOB collie, *Bob, Son of Battle*

POMPEY lapdog, *The History of Pompey the Little*

RAB Mastiff, *Rab and His Friends*

ROWF and SNITTER mongrel, fox terrier, *The Plague Dogs*

RUFF St Bernard, *Tucker's Countryside*

SEMILLANTE wolfhound, *Une Vendetta*

SERGEANT MURPHY brown dog, Richard Scarry books

SOUNDER Georgia redbone hound × bulldog, *Sounder*

TOBY-CHIEN French bulldog, *Dialogues des betes*

TRICKI-WOO Pekingese, *All Creatures Great and Small*

WEENIE pug, *Eloise*

WOLF henpecked dog, *Rip Van Winkle*

Rhyme Dogs

Edward Lear's Nonsense Rhymes included limericks about the small Ancona Dog with no Owner, the little brown Saucy-cur of Corsica, the small spotted dogs of Ryde,

There was a Young Lady of Corsica, who purchased a little brown Saucy-cur;
Which she fed upon Ham, and hot Raspberry Jam,
That expensive Young Lady of Corsica.

There was a Young Lady of Ryde, whose shoe-strings were seldom untied;
She purchased some clogs, and some small spotted dogs,
And frequently walked about Ryde.

the man-eating puppy of Leghorn and the remarkably fat cur of Kamschatka; he also defined a strange plant called the Barkia Howlaloudia. Here are some reminders of nursery rhymes and songs:

'Hark, hark, the dogs do bark,.
The beggars are coming to town
...'

'Tell-tale-tit, thy tongue is slit,
And every dog in town will get a little bit.'

'Oh where, oh where has my little dog gone?
Oh where, oh where can he be?'

'The little dog laughed to see such fun ...'

(This dog is a veiled reference to the Earl of Leicester.)

'Nick nack paddywhack, give a dog a bone ...'

'Old mother Hubbard went to the cupboard ...'

What are little boys made of, made of?
Slugs and snails and puppy-dogs' tails ...'

'The Rat, the Cat, and Lovell the Dog
Rule all England under the Hog.'

(Rat refers to Ratcliff, Cat is Catesby, and Lovell the Dog is Francis Viscount Lovell, the 'king's spaniel'. The Hog, or Boar, was the crest of Richard III. William Collingham wrote this rhyme and was put to death for doing so.)

Legend and Fable

Arthurian

CAVALL–'King Arthur's hound of greatest mouth'

HODAIN–faithful hound of banished Tristram

Welsh

GELERT–Prince Llewelyn's wolfhound, wrongfully killed by his master: a stone marks his grave near Snowdon

GWYLLGI–the enormous Dog of Darkness

Gaelic

LUATH–Cuthullin's dog in *Fingal*, said to have been tied to a stone at Dunollie Castle

MAUTHE DOG–Moddey Doo, the black spaniel which haunts Peel Castle on the Isle of Man and deters soldiers from oaths and profanity

Gelert's grave.

English

LUDLAM'S DOG–of amazing laziness, lived in Mother Ludlam's Cave

SHONY DOG–Cornish dog which barks to warn of impending storms and danger

BARGHEST–the name given in Yorkshire to a monstrous goblin-dog; such spectre-hounds appear in other regions under other names (the Demon of Tedworth, the Black Dog of Winchester, the Padfoot of Wakefield, the Trash or Striker of Lancashire, the Shuck or Shock of Norfolk and Cambridge); it has its counterparts in the Mauthe Dog, the Welsh Gwyllgi etc.

Scandinavian

GARMR–awesome blood-spattered dog chained at the gates of Hell; when the world ended he broke free and fought Tyr, the god of war, and they killed each other

RAKKAE–little dog made king of the Danes but torn to pieces by hounds squabbling over his scraps

SAUR I–dog chosen as king of Norway, reigning for three years in place of the hated King Eystein; killed protecting a lamb from a wolf

French

HERCULES or DRAGON–Montdidier's dog, who witnessed his murder and later attacked the murderer (Macaire) and fought a duel with him, pinning him by the throat until he confessed to the murder; also known as MACAIRE'S DOG, and as THE DOG OF MONTARGIS (after a mural of the duel was placed in Charles V's castle at Montargis); a 19th-century play based on the legend put a live poodle in the leading role

MOUFLAR–a mastiff whose ears were cropped so that there was less of him to be bitten, a fact which made him fearless

ROQUET—the faithful dog of St Roch

Muslim and Hindu

KASMIR—the dog of the Seven Sleepers, who kept watch for more than three hundred years

TOBIT'S DOG—who went to heaven with Tobias

SARAMA—watchdog and messenger for the great god Indra; tracked the cattle stolen by Panis from the gods

China

PAN-HU—the five-coloured dog who married the Emperor's daughter and gave her twelve children

T'IEN-KOW—the celestial dog that 'howls in the sky', and that causes the eclipse when it eats the sun or moon

Aztec

XOLOTL—twin god of Quetzalcoatl, founded a new human race with bones from the underworld.

Play Dogs

CITRON in *Les Plaideurs*

DICKIE in *La Folle de Chaillot*

LABES in Aristophanes' *Wasps*

NANA in *Peter Pan*

TOBY, the Punch and Judy scapegoat.

Painted Dogs

I would rather see the portrait of a dog that I knew than all the allegorical paintings they can show me.

Samuel Johnson,
not a noted dog-lover

Dogs have frequently been portrayed in art, usually as incidental figures because they were always to be found wherever there were people. Many artists, like many writers, were adept at

A Mythological Subject *by Piero di Cosimo.*

catching the character of a dog on canvas, whether in a hunting pack or as an accoutrement of the picture's central human subject. Some painted particular dogs, and some included their pets in their own self-portraits. Here is a randomly selective collection of painted dogs:

Hogarth 'William Hogarth With His Dog' (a pug)

Marshall 'Portrait of the Artist with His Favourite Newfoundland'

Reynolds 'Miss Bowler and Her Spaniel'

Duncan 'Bran' (Scottish deerhound)

Veronese 'The Family of Darius before Alexander' and 'An Allegory of Love' (both featuring the same dog as a symbol of fidelity)

Titian 'Bacchus and Ariadne' (small collared spaniel)

Hogarth 'Marriage a la Mode' (an assortment of dogs)

Van De Venne 'Allegory of Poverty' (shaggy white dog with very large feet)

Renoir 'Madame Charpentier and Her Children' (large shaggy black and white dog)

Lorenzetti 'Good Government' (pointing dog)

Gentile da Fabriano 'Adoration of the Magi' (large mastiff type with muzzle and heavy collar)

Paolo Uccello 'Hunt By Night' (greyhounds)

Vittore Carpaccio 'Courtesans' (begging white dog and a wolf-faced dog)

Jan Van Eyck 'Giovanna Cenami and Giovanni Arnolfini' (griffon type)

A Hound and Bitch in a Landscape *by George Stubbs.*

Pomeranian Bitch and Puppy *by Gainsborough.*

Hans Memlinc 'Bathsheba' (poodle type)

Hieronymus Bosch 'Pedlar' (curly-tailed mongrel)

Master of the Life of the Virgin 'Conversion of St Hubert' (three types–hound, spaniel, greyhound)

Pieter Bruegel 'Hunters in the Snow' (hounds, greyhounds, terriers)

Piero Di Cosimo 'A Mythological Subject' (large, mournful dog in foreground–Laelaps, in the classical legend of Procris and Cephalus)

Jacopo Bassano 'Good Samaritan' and other paintings (spaniel or pointer types)

Mathieu Le Nain 'Peasants' Meal' (hairy terrier)

Murillo 'Boys with Fruit' (mongrel)

Watteau 'Enseigne de Gersaint' (dog with fleas)

Tiepolo 'Apotheosis of the Prince Bishop' (large dog with long, thin tail and feathered hound ears)

Gainsborough 'Pomeranian Bitch and Puppy'

Goya 'Parasol' (lapdog)

Reynolds 'Nelly O'Brien' (Bolognese, bichon or poodle)

Zoffany 'Family Group' (bourgeois pet!)

Rubens 'The Chateau de Steen' (sportsman's spaniel)

Cuyp 'A Hilly River Landscape' (playing dogs).

Famous animal artists such as Stubbs, Bewick and Reinagle painted many a dog, but there is perhaps one artist above all who is remembered for his dogs – he painted them, he adored them, and he knew a great deal about dog psychology. On one occasion he was asked to tame a savage dog kept on a chain, which no one could come near. He approached it on all fours, growling, snarling and snapping, and the terrified dog snapped its chain, leapt over the wall and fled, howling, never to be seen again. The artist was Landseer.

Landseer's Models

BRUTUS, his own rough white terrier mongrel

LASSIE and MYRTLE, his Scottish sheepdog and retriever

BRECHIN, Landseer's less than intelligent dog who was drowned at sea with a tin can stuck on the end of his nose (he had retrieved it)

TRACKER, another of the artist's own dogs

LION, a St Bernard (or Alpine mastiff as then known), the largest of its kind in England (6 ft 4 in (101.6 cm) long, 2 ft 7 in (78.74 cm) high at the dip of its back and the first of Landseer's pictures exhibited. He was 13 when he painted it. LION and CAESAR featured two or three years later in 'Alpine Mastiffs Reanimating a Distressed Traveller'

CAESAR, son of LION

MAIDA, Sir Walter Scott's famous and much painted deerhound

GINGER and SPICE, Scott's Dandie Dinmonts

BRAN and OSCAR, deerhounds

BOXER, Charles Dickens' dog

ODIN, a bloodhound

COUNTESS, Jacob Bell's bloodhound which was painted either just dead or just dying

TRIM, William Wells's favourite spaniel

FIDO, Miss Eliza Peel's spaniel in 'Beauty's Bath'

BONEY, the Duke of Devonshire's Blenheim spaniel

MUSTARD, Sir Francis Chantrey's favourite dog, son of PEPPER

GRAFTON (bloodhound) and SCRATCH (terrier) in 'Dignity and Impudence'

PAUL PRY, the Newfoundland in perhaps the most famous Landseer painting, 'A Distinguished Member of the Humane Society'

JOLLY, the last dog painted by Landseer, owned by old Mrs Pritchard

Landseer's Royal models

CAIRNACH
DANDY
DASH (DASBY)
EOS
FLORA
HECTOR
ISLAY
LAMBKIN
LOOTIE
NELSON
WALDMAN and DACKEL

Landseer's very early dogs

Study of foxhound from life (when he was 5)

'Head of Pointer Bitch and Puppy' (aged 13)

'Fighting Dogs Getting Wind' (first picture sold–for 30 guineas– when he was already known as 'the dog-boy')

'The Cat Disturbed' (featuring BRUTUS)

'Lioness and Bitch' (lion cub suckled by bitch)

In 1821, at the age of 19, Landseer wrote down a 'list of pictures

Sir Walter Scott in the Rhymer's Glen *by Landseer.*

painted which I have been paid for', including:

'Fighting Dogs' (£31.10s)

'Poney and Dog' (£4.4s)

'Plummer's Dog' (£21)

'Alpine Mastiffs' (£180)

Landseer Paintings:

'Old English Bloodhound' (his first Woburn picture)

'Rat Catchers' (featuring BRUTUS, VIXEN and BOXER)

'The Larder Invaded' (BRUTUS)

'The Faithful Hound' (painted in 1830 as his diploma picture to become a full Royal Acadamician)

'High Life' and 'Low Life' (deerhound and rolypoly

butcher's dog–almost his last picture of a 'non-aristocratic' dog)

'On Trust' (Princess Mary of Cambridge with a Newfoundland balancing a biscuit on its nose)

'The Sutherland Children' (dogs with fawn)

'Trial by Jury: or Laying Down the Law' (pontificating dogs, one of a satirical series)

'A Cross of a Dog and a Fox' (result of freak mating)

'Comical Dogs' (tykes dressed up)

'Good Doggie' (pious pomeranian at prayer)

'Jack In Office' (smug terrier guarding meat-barrow from four hungry mongrels)

'Sir Walter Scott in the Rhymer's Glen' (with MAIDA and GINGER and SPICE)

'Suspense' (bloodhound, blood and cavalier's plume)

'Attachment' (terrier bitch guarding dead man in the Welsh mountains, based on true story where she stayed with his body for three months)

'Saved!' (Newfoundland with little girl rescued from the sea, dedicated to the Royal Humane Society)

'The Connoisseurs' (self portrait with LASSIE and MYRTLE).

It was said of Landseer: 'Not a dog in London but knows him.' He also knew all the dog thieves and could always find someone's lost pet! In a potted biography, it was declared that his birthplace was 'most probably near the Isle of Dogs' and mentioned his 'dogged determination to outstrip all competitors in the canine race ...' Awful puns seemed to be tailor-made for Landseer, and one publication produced a eulogy to this 'dog-fancier' which ended:

There's not a dog but owes you
  more, I trow,
Than e'er he owed his pa
Or his dog-ma
And not a cur that meets
You in the streets
But ought to make you a profound
  bow-Wow!

and added as a tailpiece:

Excuse these Doggerel rhymes,
  my dear Landseer.

Heraldic Dogs

The most common types of dogs found in heraldry are:

Alant or **Aland** (crop-eared mastiff)

Greyhound (14th-century symbol of fidelity)

Irish Wolfhound (arms of ancient Irish kings–the breed was said to be 'gentle when stroked, fierce when provoked')

Talbot (the hound of ancient times which in the early days of heraldry represented the genus Dog–a strong, thickset dog looking like a cross between a hound and a mastiff, with hanging hound ears, a foxhound type of tail in a semi-circular curve, combined with the powerful limbs and slobbering jowl of a mastiff)

Other dogs include:

Alaskan Malamute (Yukon Territory crest)

Bulldog

Kenet (little tracking dog)

Mauleverer (running greyhound)

Pointer

Ratch Hound (small dog of the beagle type)

Some Family Dogs:

Baron Alington (two silver **Talbots** with red roses in mouths)

Heraldic sea-dog.

Harris (commoner with **Cornish Sea-dog!**)

Kenet (**Kenet**, 13th century)

Talbot of Cumberland (**Talbot** dog, of course)

Talbot of Shrewsbury likewise, but **Talbot** of Lancashire preferred three purple squirrels

Viscount Hereford (**Talbot** head)

Woode (John) of Kent (**Alaund**, 15th-century shield)

The **Greyhound** is in a class of its own as the most common heraldic dog. For example, the Wiltshire town of MARLBOROUGH includes in its arms two greyhounds as supporters, symbolic of the forestry and hunting privileges the ancient royal borough had enjoyed and reminding the town of local sports in later days when greyhound coursing was popular.

The greyhound was also a very royal dog:

Charles V of France two blue greyhounds

Edward VI Royal supporters were two silver greyhounds

Elizabeth Widville, Queen of **Edward IV** Silver greyhound, collared and chained

Henry II of France two greyhounds

Henry VII Royal badge showed white greyhound courant coloured azure (denoting his maternal descent from John, Earl of Somerset). The king's royal supporters were two silver greyhounds, representing the white greyhound of Neville.

Henry VIII had the same badge and supporters

James II Supporters were two greyhounds sejant adorsed, each holding an ostrich feather

Mary, and **James I** Royal supporters were greyhounds

1st Earl of Panmure two greyhounds as supporters because he gained recognition from James IV when he entertained the king with sport on the moors of Monroben

Philippe VI of France two greyhounds.

Dog Stars

We know that the tail must wag the dog,
for the horse is drawn by the cart,
But the Devil whoops as he whooped of old:
'It's pretty, but is it Art?'

Rudyard Kipling
The Conundrum of the Workshops

ASTA a schnauzer in the book but a wire-haired terrier on celluloid whose real name was SKIPPY–in

the 'Third Man' series with
William Powell and Myrna Loy

BENJI shaggy mongrel rescued
from an animal shelter–probably
cocker spaniel × poodle ×
schnauzer; also starred as
HIGGINS in television series
'Petticoat Junction'; retired at 17
and was replaced by one of his
own female pups

BULLET Roy Rogers' German
shepherd dog

CHINOOK white German
shepherd, famous Yukon mountie
dog, real name HARVEY, beautiful
dark eyes, tended to bite
everybody, later starred in series
'Corky and White Shadow'

CLEO television's 'talking' basset
hound

DAISY hairy mongrel in the
'Blondie' films, based on a comic
strip

DUKE Great Dane with cowboy
Tom Mix and his horse Tony

JEAN a collie, and America's first
film dog in preference to an
awkward pomeranian

LASSIE *the* rough collie, in fact
played by a male dog called PAL
in films and on radio, and by his
male descendants on television
and in later films

LAUGHING GRAVY mongrel with
Laurel and Hardy

LUKE English pit bull terrier
given to Fatty Arbuckle's wife
Minta; acted for the Sennett 'zoo'
and later saved Minta's mother
from drowning

MIKE stars with Nick Nolte, Bette
Midler and Richard Dreyfuss in
Down And Out In Beverly Hills.
He is a Scottish border collie with
one blue and one brown eye and
has appeared on a number of

prestigious American chat shows

NEIL St Bernard in television's
'Topper' series–a ghost dog who
drank martinis

NIKON Russian star in *A Car, a
Fiddle and a Dog*

OLD YELLER ugly mongrel with a
missing ear in Texas frontier
drama, real name SPIKE

PROPS backstage dog who
happened to save a baby in a
runaway pram on set and became
a filmstar himself with the Gish
sisters–his greatest role was with
Dorothy Gish in *The Little Yank*
and he was a fine ham actor who
knew how to get sympathy off the
set as well as on it

RIN TIN TIN the most famous
German shepherd dog of them all,
rescued as a puppy by an
American airman from an
abandoned German dugout in
France in World War I and named
after a lucky doll–brilliant at
stunts, brilliant at acting, and
insured for a hundred thousand
dollars; he died in the presence of
Jean Harlow and was succeeded
in his roles by his son and
grandsons

ROVER collie—the world's first dog star, real name BLAIR, appeared in *Rescued By Rover* a seven-minute drama by Cecil Hepworth in 1907.

RUSTY German shepherd, real name FLAME, a top performer in the 1940s and early 1950s, who also played SHEP

SAVAGE SAM bluetick trailhound, son of OLD YELLER

SCRAPS Charlie Chaplin's mongrel, real name BROWNIE, who had been rescued from the dog-catcher and went on to star not only in *A Dog's Life* but in 50 two-reelers

SOLO and HAVOC wild dogs in Hugo van Lawick's television film *The Wild Dogs of Africa*

STRONGHEART German shepherd—first feature film with a canine hero, originally trained to kill as a police dog; he was a dog of very high intelligence indeed who starred first in *The Silent Call* and was also the first to portray a guide dog for the blind on screen

TOTO little black dog in *The Wizard of Oz*

Toto and Judy Garland in The Wizard of Oz.

YUKON KING husky or malamute which barked before each episode of the radio show *Challenge of the Yukon.*

Disney Dogs

GOOFY
PLUTO
LADY and THE TRAMP

Lady and the Tramp.

WET
CEMENT

Twelve of the 101 Dalmatians.

THE SHAGGY DOG
GREYFRIARS BOBBY
101 DALMATIANS, including:
CADPIG
LUCKY
MISSIS
PERDITA
PONGO
COLONEL the sheepdog

The PATSY Awards

The American Humane
Association in Hollywood began
making awards to animal actors in
1951. The PATSY award was
originally for the Picture Animal
Top Star of the Year but in 1958
PATSY extended to television–
Performing Animal Television
Star of the Year. The winners have
included everything from hawks
and dolphins to camels and
coyotes, with a lot of dogs in

between. Here are the dogs:

PATSY Hall of Fame

1973 LASSIE, *Lassie*
1975 BENJI, *Benji*
1977 SCRUFFY, *The Ghost and
Mrs Muir*
1984 HARRY, a black
labrador/Great Dane mix,
owned and trained by Karl
Lewis Miller

PATSY Film Dogs

1951 FLAME, *My Pal* series
LASSIE, *Challenge of
Lassie*
1952 CHINOOK, *Yukon
Manhunt*
CORKY, *Behave Yourself*
1953 TRAMP JR, *Room For One
More*
CHINOOK, *Yukon Gold*
1954 SAM, *Hondo*
BARON, *Back to God's
Country*

1955 SHEP, *A Bullet is Waiting*

1956 WILDFIRE, *It's a Dog's Life*
FARO, *The Kentuckian*

1957 LADY, *Goodbye, My Lady*
BASCOM, *Hollywood or Bust*

1958 SPIKE, *Old Yeller*
KELLY, *Kelly and Me*

1959 KING, *The Proud Rebel*

1960 SHAGGY, *The Shaggy Dog*

1961 SPIKE, *Dog of Flanders*
SKIP, *Visit to a Small Planet*

1962 PETE, *The Silent Call*

1963 BIG RED, *Big Red*

1964 TOM DOOLEY, *Savage Sam*
PLUTO, *My Six Loves*

1965 STORM, *Goodbye Charlie*
JUNIOR, *Island of the Blue Dolphins*

1967 DUKE, *The Ugly Dachshund*

Scene from Call of the Wild.

PATSY Television Dogs

have included:

LASSIE and LASSIE'S PUPS
CLEO
RIN TIN TIN
ASTA
JASPER
TRAMP
LORD NELSON
HIGGINS
SCRUFFY
PAX
FAROUK
CAESAR

PATSY Canine Category Winners

In 1976 the PATSY awards were given to categories of animal rather than to film or television performers. Canine Category winners have included:

TIGER, *The Boy and His Dog*

GUS, *Won Ton Ton*

FIVE DOBERMANNS, *The Amazing Dobermann*

BOURBON, *Call of the Wild*

Scene from Challenge to Lassie.

KODIAC AND SLED TEAM, *Call of the Wild*

SAM, a golden labrador, *Sam* series

TUNDRA, *Love Boat*

FOLSOM, *Body Double*

PATSY Craven and Human/Animal Bond Awards

FLAME and Frank Barnes, owner and trainer

SANDY, from the Broadway production *Annie*

OJ, 'a dog/mutt' owned and trained by Bob Weatherwax

SNEAKERS, a puppy, *Highway to Heaven*, owned and supplied by Gary Gero, trained by Roger Schumacher and Gwen Johnson.

The Acting Alsatians

German shepherd dogs seem to be favourites in the film world because of their trainability and good looks. Apart from those already mentioned, star alsatians included:

ACE
BOOTS
BRAVEHEART
FLASH
GINGER (collie cross)
RUSTY (cross)
THUNDER
ZORRO

Star Trainers

Frank Barnes (FLAME/RUSTY, GOLDEN BOY JUNIOR/JAY-ARE, Jay-Are's stand-in HEY YOU, GRAY SHADOW)

Rand Brooks (BEARHEART)

Lee Duncan (RIN TIN TIN and successors)

Henry East (ASTA)

Frank Inn (BENJI/HIGGINS, JEEP, ASTA, DAISY, LASSIE, CLEO)

Earl Johnson (BULLET)

Rennie Renfro (DAISY)

Rudd Weatherwax (LASSIE, WIGGLES, DAISY, ASTA, CORKY and many, many more)

Sam Williamson/Duke York (CHINOOK)

Petra

BBC Television's favourite and longest running children's TV programme must surely be *Blue Peter*, and the programme's most famous dog must be PETRA.

PETRA, black and brown prick-eared mongrel, joined 1962, made 1,192 appearances (550 hours of television), retired 30 June, 1977; died 18 September, 1977, aged 14 years 10 months. Statue by William Timyn in bronze at BBC's Television Centre, inside main gates. Her name was chosen from 10,000 suggestions sent in by viewers.

PETRA's famous friends:

Princess Anne, Prince Andrew, Prince Edward, Viscount Linley, Lady Sarah Armstrong-Jones, Yehudi Menuhin, James Galway, Ringo Starr, David Cassidy, Dame Margot Fonteyn, The Hollies, members of the British Everest Expedition 1975 (Chris Bonington, Doug Scott, Dougal Haston, Mick Burke) and many more.

PETRA's potential studs:

TONTO (bull terrier)

TRISKA (border collie)

WHIMPEY (smooth-haired terrier)

LUKE (golden cocker spaniel)

BELLMAN (beagle–voted outright choice by viewers but he did not succeed with Petra)

MOSS (Shetland sheepdog chosen by Petra)

PETRA's puppies (born 9 September 1965):

KIM and PETER (to children's homes)

BRUCE and REX (to farm homes)

PRINCE (to an old people's home)

ROVER (regimental mascot)

PATCH (*A Blue Peter* dog, died May 1971)

CANDY who had three pups herself:
BRANDY
DANDY
MANDY who had two pups:
ZEBEDEE, ZABADAK

CHANG (St Bernard belonging to George du Maurier, often a model for *Punch* and other sketches)

CHOLMONDELEY

DAISY

FRED BASSET

GORGON

HUCKLEBERRY HOUND

KELLY

MARMADUKE

MILOU

NAPOLEON

OFFISA BULL PUPP

PEGLET PETE

PLUTO

SANDY

SCOOBY DOO

SNOOPY and friends

TIGE

TIPPIE

ZERO

Cartoon and Comic Dogs

BEAUREGARD BUGLEBOY

BINGO

Puppets

ROWLF

SOOTY

TOBY

Chart Dogs

Dog Songs

Bird Dog	Everly Brothers
Chihuahua	Bow Wow Wow
Diamond Dogs	David Bowie
Dog Eat Dog	Adam and the Ants
Dogs	The Who
Hot Dog	Shakin' Stevens
Hound Dog	Procol Harum
Hounds of Love	Kate Bush

How Much Is That Doggie In The Window?	Lita Roza
I Love My Dog	Cat Stevens
Lonely Pup (In A Christmas Shop)	Adam Faith
Matchstick Men And Matchstick Cats and Dogs	Brian and Michael
Me And You And A Dog Named Boo	Lobo
Puppy Love	Donny Osmond
Salty Dog	Elvis Presley
Snoopy Vs The Red Baron	Hotshots
The Puppy Song	David Cassidy
Walking My Cat Named Dog	Norma Tanega

Dog Bands

Bonzo Dog Doo Dah Band
Bow Wow Wow
The Corgi's
Three Dog Night

and finally ... Singing Dogs an
American canine vocal group!

Advertising Dogs

SANDY, basset hound (Hush Puppies)

DUKE the Old English sheepdog (Dulux paints)

MACK BULLDOG, truck symbol, World War I

NIPPER, His Master's Voice

SCOTTISH TERRIERS for Black & White Scotch Whisky

SCRUFFY, Chuckwagon dog food (1974 special PATSY award)

ST BERNARD for St Bruno tobacco.

Sandy.

108

And More Dog Stars

DRAGON, who went on stage in 1775 with Thomas Weston in *The Rival Candidates*. Weston, son of a cook in the kitchen of King George II, was a well-known actor but when in one performance he refused to appear with the dog (which stood as high as his waist) fruit and bottles were hurled on to the stage.

ZOPPICO, a poodle-like dog which performed for the emperor Vespasian two thousand years ago (according to Plutarch). It chewed a piece of meat but suddenly had a fit, opening its eyes wide, and, giving a death rattle, fell to the ground as if poisoned to death. When its audience applauded it sprung to life again, wagging its tail furiously.

Many unremembered dogs have performed with street acrobats and in circuses. Dalmatians were often clowns' dogs and poodles were circus performers.

Celestial Dogs

CANIS MAJOR is the GREAT DOG, a constellation just below and behind the heels of Orion the Hunter. CANIS MINOR, the LITTLE DOG, also follows Orion and is separated from its big brother by the Milky Way.

CYNOSURE, the Pole Star, seen by all observers and thus the centre of attention. From the Greek for DOG's TAIL

SIRIUS is the principal star in CANIS MAJOR and is the brightest star in the heavens. Its name has connotations with the Greek word for 'scorching' and the Arabic 'glittering one'. Its appearance in the morning with the sun heralded forty days of strong, hot winds in Greece, and if it appeared misty it promised a plague of locusts. But Zoroastrians appointed Sirius as a guard in the heavens, and in the Avesta it is called TISTRYA and is 'the bright and happy star, that gives happy dwelling'. For the Egyptians it was the most important star of all: appearing with the sun as the Nile was rising, it heralded the flooding that would bring renewed fertility to the land. For the Romans, the rising of the star marked the commencement of their new year. It was the 'second sun' of the heavens, but the Greeks considered it the 'evil star' which 'parches head and knees'.

PROCYON, so called because it rose before SIRIUS, is the principal star in CANIS MAJOR. Like SIRIUS, it was one of the hounds of Orion. It became MAERA, the dog of Icarius, when Bootes became Icarius and Virgo represented his daughter Erigone.

Space Dogs

For my part, I travel not to go anywhere, but to go. I travel for travel's sake. The great affair is to move.

R L Stevenson
Travels with a Donkey

LAIKA was the first living creature to orbit the earth. Also known as CURLY or LITTLE LEMON, she was a typical Russian spitz type weighing about 11 pounds. She was launched in Sputnik II on 3 November, 1957, strapped in and wired up with sensors. She seemed to cope well enough with this first space flight but unfortunately re-entry was

not at that time practicable and she died when her oxygen supply ran out after ten days in orbit.

BELKA and STRELKA were the first living creatures to return alive from space. Of a similar type to Laika, they took off in Sputnik V on 19 August, 1960, and completed seventeen orbits of the earth in about twenty-five hours. They returned safe and sound, and later on were able to produce normal puppies. One of Strelka's pups, PUSHINKA, was presented to President John F Kennedy's wife, Jackie.

IKAR is not a flying dog but is owned by Cosmonaut V Sevastyanov.

LAIKA was also the name given to an English white boxer bitch. Born in 1967, she was owned by Major C J T Davey who took her with him on most military activities including ballooning. H A B Gerard A Heineken (G-BCFZ) had a two-storey basket with room for twelve on the flight deck and for twenty on the other deck, including LAIKA who would sit on the wicker bench and watch the world pass by through the window. As her owner says, 'After a flight she would express the general elation of the crew by

tearing about in a mad career'. She also flew in H A B Silver Jubilee, a four-man craft. She did not, however, like flying at above 5,000 feet: she would lie prone, look mournful and sometimes moan quietly – showing the typical balloonist's feeling of insecurity at such an unnatural altitude. She died in 1979.

FLIGHTY was LAIKA's successor: she was a brindle boxer born in 1981. Major Davey says that her precipitate enthusiasm was such that she always had to be kept on the lead. On one occasion the balloon made a false landing and took off again, but FLIGHTY had already slipped her collar and disappeared. They landed later a few fields away, and the breathless boxer was there to greet them. Unfortunately she was too bumptious to continue as a balloonist and now lives in London with all four paws firmly on the ground.

Explorers

Naturally dogs have featured on all the famous Arctic journeys. Captain Scott took some samoyeds with him to the Antarctic, but the first lot were weak and had to be shot and on another attempt the dogs had to be sent back to Australia at the first advance station. Dogs have, however, proved invaluable in the Arctic and some famous achievements are listed on page 76. Nansen's book, *Farthest North*, and a book published in 1853 by Lt William Hulme Hooper, RN, both tell wondrous tales of North Pole dogs. Here are some more of them:

BALTO, a black Alaskan malamute, was the famous leader of Gunnar Kasson's dog team which brought life-saving anti-diphtheria serum to Nome, Alaska, in 1925. The serum was taken in relays over a distance of 675 miles (1,086 km) and Balto led for the final 60 miles (96 km) in the teeth of an 80 mph blizzard. A statue of the dog was erected in New York City's Central Park in December of that year.

BARBEKARK was an Eskimo dog who was a favourite of Captain Hall. The dog once killed a deer, took only one morsel from its neck and then went home and fetched his master to the carcase. (The dog's brother was a distinguished seal catcher: he was the team's lead dog and once took off at full speed after a seal, sledge and all. He caught his prey by a hind flipper just as it was plunging into the water, and with the help of the team he dragged it back on to the ice for his master.) Barbekark was a very intelligent dog, not to say cunning. Hall tells of a new trick at feeding time, when the team would receive small dried fish called capelins. The dogs stood in a circle around their master, who fed them one by one. Barbekark soon learned to take his capelin, sneak behind his fellows and squeeze back into the circle a few dogs further on so that he was fed again. When the first attempt was successful, he moved three or four more places round the circle and achieved a third helping. But Hall got wise to the trick and passed him by on the next meal, although Barbekark changed position several times. Finally the dog withdrew from the circle and crowded up against

Hall's legs, looking up at him with the greatest repentance.

IGLOO was no wolf dog—he was a fox terrier who went with Admiral Byrd on his first Antarctic expedition in 1928–30. He was given lined boots, a camel-hair coat covering his legs, and a wool-

lined sleeping crate at the foot of Byrd's bed. He was always game for a go at the large Eskimo dogs and 'no doubt he believed he was a great fighter because we saved his life so often'.

Other Exploring Dogs

BOBBIE was a young female collie. Her family moved from Ohio to a new home in Oregon which the dog had never been to. She wandered off on the journey during a stop in Indiana and turned up in Oregon three months later.

LEONCICO was a yellow hound belonging to Balboa the Spanish explorer, with whom he travelled across the Isthmus of Panama to the Pacific in 1513. He drew the pay of a crossbowman.

HOBO was a much travelled dog, living up to his name. He turned up in 1957 at a railroad yard in Hopewell, Virginia, and thereafter he travelled thousands of miles either in the cab or on the catwalks. He always returned to Hopewell as his base.

OWNEY did even better and in the 19th century he was claimed to be the most travelled dog in history, according to the US Post Office. He came in out of the cold one day as a puppy and found himself in a post office in Albany, New York, in 1888. When he got bored of watching the mail sacks being loaded on to railway cars he disappeared, but he returned and was given a collar and tag asking postal workers to stamp on it the names of the places he reached. He was given a lifetime pass to ride on any US mail car. He reached Alaska in 1895, went down the Pacific Coast to Tacoma and then followed the mail sack up a gangplank on the SS Victoria, bound for Japan, where he was presented to the Mikado, decorated and given an honorary passport. The Emperor of China honoured him in the same fashion. He went through the Suez Canal and back across the Atlantic to his home base, having accumulated two hundred medals on his travels. He later died after a dog fight; his body was sent to the taxidermist and he was put on display in the Postal Museum, Washington DC, along with all his medals and stamped tags.

SCANNON was a black Newfoundland on the Lewis and Clark expedition exploring the Louisiana Purchase. He belonged to Meriwether Lewis and acted as watchdog and hunter (favourite prey included rabbits, geese and swimming deer). He saved Lewis and Clark from a buffalo bull in full charge by heading him off. The dog was stolen by Indians in 1806 but they released him as soon as they found themselves being pursued.

Intrepid Dogs

Is thy servant a dog, that he should do this great thing?
2 Kings VIII 13

BILLY was a famous terrier who killed a hundred large rats in 5 minutes 30 seconds (in a pit), and later reduced his time by 22 seconds. When he was old with only two teeth left and one eye missing, the owner of a Berkshire bitch bet fifty sovereigns that his

bitch would beat Billy's time on fifty rats. Billy achieved his full kill in 5 minutes 6 seconds, but the bitch gave up after killing only thirty. Billy's hundred-rat record in Westminster Pit was depicted in a coloured aquatint in Pierce Egan's *Book of Sports*, 1882.

DOX was a German shepherd dog detective in Italy and as clever as they come—he could untie knots, unload pistols, and remember a wanted man six years after the fugitive had eluded him. He competed in Europe's annual police-dog matches and first won the crown in 1953, successfully defending it for several years against other famous police dogs like REX of Scotland Yard and Xorro of Paris. Dox won four gold medals, twenty-seven silvers, and had seven bullet-wound scars by the time he was 14 years old. Owned and trained by Police Sergeant Giovanni Maimone, he saved a child from being run over by a car, tracked down a lost skier, kept twelve suspects at bay with raised arms until help arrived, caught a burglar after a long chase with one of his legs shattered by a bullet, and was famous for solving crimes all on his own.

JACK was a dalmatian, the mascot of Brooklyn's Engine Company 105 in New York. He rolled a fallen child out of the way of the firetruck as it accelerated out of the station, and received a Medal of Valour.

NICK CARTER was a bloodhound whose tracking resulted in the conviction of more than six hundred criminals. He could pick up a trail four days old and could track a man on horseback. He was owned and trained by Captain Volney G. Mullikan of Kentucky and West Virginia.

TREP (short for INTREPID) is a golden retriever trained as a sniffer dog to scent out illegal drugs. His owner, Tom Kazo, was a police officer in Florida when he began to train the dog in 1973, and within two months Trep had sniffed out a haul of one and a half tons of hashish in the bulkheads of a sloop. The following year he found cocaine in a doll clutched by a young girl leaving a plane in Miami. By 1979 he was responsible for a hundred arrests and the recovery of narcotics worth more than sixty-three million dollars. In the *Guinness*

Book of Records (1978 edition) Trep was given the task of detecting ten hidden drugs packets at a demonstration in a school. He found all eleven of them!

Weird and Wonderful Dogs

As who should say, 'I am Sir Oracle,
And when I ope my lips let no dog bark'.

Shakespeare
Merchant of Venice

Many dogs are claimed to be able to talk, count, thought-read, read, predict and so on, and many of the stories could well be true. Here are some, true or not:

BERGANZA was a fictional talking dog in Cervantes' *Colloquy of the Dogs* who told his life story to another watchdog. He joined a drummer to perform tricks and went on to become a comedian with a theatrical troupe.

BLITZ was a 'talking' German shepherd dog belonging to a school custodian in the Bronx: he would tell him 'I want a hamburger' or 'want out' etc.

CHRIS THE WONDER DOG, owned by George Wood in the 1950s, was thoroughly researched. He responded to verbal questions by pawing his owner's arm, and could guess hidden symbols accurately.

GYP, a German shepherd dog owned by Herbert Neff of Knoxville, Tennessee, left home in a huff when the family's second baby was born but returned without fail on Christmas day for the next ten years.

ROLF was an Airedale from Mannheim who understood arithmetic and learned the letters of the alphabet. Using numbers to represent letters, he would tap out messages with his paw. He is said to have predicted an earthquake in 1912, and to have answered a woman who had asked what she could do for him by saying, 'Wag your tail.'

LOLA was sired by ROLF the Airedale and used his methods to predict the weather.

KURWENAL was a dachshund who was also supposed to be a talker and who, along with ROLF and LOLA, inspired Graham Greene to write in his essay 'Great Dogs of Weimar' that dogs, 'solid, well-meaning, reliable . . . seem to possess all the least attractive human virtues. What bores, I have sometimes thought, if they could speak, and now my most appalling conjectures have been confirmed.'

MR LUCKY was a talking Boston terrier with a voice like a talking doll, thin and high, although his normal bark was deep.

MISSIE, Boston terrier with deep cobalt-blue eyes, the Clairvoyant of Denver in the 1960s. She predicted the times of certain events by moving the hands of a cardboard clock, and she indicated the time of her own death exactly.

PEPE was a talking Chihuahua who 'sung' his words and who appeared on television several times in California.

PROFESSOR DUNCAN had a troupe of performing rough collies which acted out an elaborate routine: they were a fire brigade called to a burning house, where, while rescuing one of their

number posing as a child, another one 'sacrificed his life' in the attempt, and the troupe buried him with full ceremony.

RAGS was part Scottie, part wire-haired terrier. He turned up in Sing-Sing prison in 1929 and remained there for 12 years (voluntarily). He performed tricks to cheer up the prisoners but ignored warders and guards. Scrupulously fair, he attended a different table at mess every day. He was particularly sensitive to depressed prisoners, and spent a whole night with a potential suicide growling at him to prevent him hanging himself.

STRONGHEART, the famous film dog, would perform a pantomime to J Allen Boone explaining exactly what he wanted or why he was behaving in a certain way. It was a two-way communication between man and dog.

There was a SPITZ who acted as a night nurse for her diabetic mistress: she slept in the crook of her arm and woke instantly if her breathing changed indicating a coma. The spitz would immediately go and wake the woman's daughter in the next room.

In a Word...

DOG, n. A kind of additional or subsidiary Deity designed to catch the overflow and surplus of the worship. This Divine Being in some of his smaller and silkier incarnations takes, in the affection of Woman, the place to which there is no human male aspirant. The Dog is a survival—an anachronism. He toils not, neither does he spin, yet Solomon in all his glory never lay upon a door-mat all day long, sun-soaked and fly-fed and fat, while his master worked for the means wherewith to purchase an idle wag of the Solomonic tail, seasoned with a look of tolerant recognition.

Ambrose Bierce
The Devil's Dictionary

Give a breed a name...

Many breeds have more than one name:

Affenpinscher Monkey terrier

Afghan Hound Greyhound in pyjamas, Afghan or Persian greyhound, Barukhzy hound, Cabul dog

Airedale Broken-haired, Working, Waterside or Old English terrier

Australian Cattle Dog Heeler

Basenji Congo dog

Bedlington Terrier Gypsy dog

Black and Tan Terrier Manchester terrier

Bloodhound Draughthound, Sluithound

Border Collie Old-fashioned sheepdog, Farm collie, Working collie

Borzoi Russian wolfhound

Chinese Crested Dog Turkish naked dog

Chow Chow Chow, Wolf dog

Clydesdale Terrier Paisley terrier

Dalmatian Dally, Firehouse dog, Spotted dick, Plum pudding dog

Dingo Warragal or Native dog

English Setter Laverack

English Toy Terrier Toy Manchester, Toy black-and-tan or Miniature black-and-tan terrier, or 'Apple-headed 'uns'

Fila Brasileira Dog of Acores

Finnish Spitz Barking bird dog

German Shepherd Dog Alsatian wolf dog

Giant Schnauzer Riesenschnauzer, Munchen dog, Russian bear schnauzer

Grand Griffon Vendeen Chien blanc du roi

Great Dane Apollo of dogs, Grand Danois, Dogue Allemande, German mastiff, Vertagri, Bearhound, Tiger mastiff

Irish Setter Big red

Irish Water Spaniel Tweed, North or McCarthy spaniel

Keeshond Dutch barge dog,

Clark Gable and his award-winning Irish Red Setter.

Fik, Foxdog. Overweight pomeranian

Kelpie Australian collie

Lhasa Apso Tibetan apso, Lhasa terrier, Bhuteen terrier

Lurcher Poacher's dog

Maltese Melita

Mexican Hairless Dog Chinese hairless dog, Pelon dog

Norwich Terrier Trumpington, Jones or Cantal terrier

Old English Mastiff Bandog, Tie dog

Old English Sheepdog Drover's dog, Bobtailed sheepdog, Smithfield dog (when crossed with collie), Bobtail

Papillon Butterfly spaniel, Squirrel dog

Pomeranian Foxdog

Poodle Caniche (from canard = duck)

Rhodesian Ridgeback Rhodesian lion dog, Safari dog

Rough Collie Scotch collie

Saluki Arabian or Eastern greyhound, Shami, Sleughi or Slughi

Scottish Deerhound Scotch or Highland greyhound, Northern hound, Fleethound, Rough greyhound

Scottish Terrier Aberdeen terrier

Shetland Sheepdog Sheltie

Shih-tzu Lion dog

Silky Terrier Sidney terrier

Staffordshire Bull Terrier Bull and terrier dog, Half and half dog, Pit dog, Pit bull terrier

Staffordshire Terrier American pit bull terrier, Yankee terrier

Tibetan Terrier Double chrysanthemum dog

Vizsla Hungarian yellow pointer

Welsh Springer Spaniel Starter

West Highland Terrier Roseneath or Poltalloch terrier

Yorkshire Terrier Scotch or Rough terrier

Why 'Affenpinscher'?

Affenpinscher affe = 'monkey', pinscher = 'terrier'

Basenji Bantu word meaning 'native' or 'of the bush'

Basset bas = 'low'

Beagle Old French beegueulle = 'clamourer'

Boxer so called from its habit of starting to play or fight by striking out with its forepaws

Cairn so called because it was small enough to squeeze into the cairns (heaps of stones) where its prey took refuge

Sir Walter Scott *by William Allan, with his Dandie Dinmonts.*

Cocker 'woodcocker', i.e. a dog used to flush woodcock

Collie possibly connected with the word col ('black')–the dogs were used to herd a dark 19th-century sheep known in Scotland as the colley

Corgi corr = 'dwarf', ci = 'dog'

Dachshund dachs = 'badger', hund = 'dog'

Dandie Dinmont named after a character in a Scott novel

Dobermann name of German tax collector who created breed

Harrier hare chaser

Husky either from the Chukchi or Chuch Eskimoes of the Kolyma River area in Siberia, or from the word tuski, a fast sledge pulled by up to 20 dogs

Jack Russell named after Rev John Russell, breeder

Kuvasz 'protector'

Lhasa Apso Lhasa is the capital

of Tibet; apso is possibly from abso seng kye = 'barking sentinel lion dog'

Malamute named after the Mahlemut tribe of Alaska

Mastiff possibly the Latin massivus = 'massive', or Old French mastin = 'tame' or mestif = 'mongrel', or derived from Low Latin masnata = 'household' (i.e. household dog), or (improbably) from the words mase or master theefe = 'terror to thieves'

Norsk Buhund bu = 'cattle'

Pinscher 'terrier'

Pug a word applied to goblins, snub noses, pet monkeys and as a general term of endearment; some say the dog is named from the Latin pugnus = 'fist' because its profile resembles a fist!

Saluki possibly after the vanished town of Saluk or Salug in southern Arabia, or Selenkia in the Syrian Empire, or from a word meaning 'noble'

Samoyed named after a Siberian tribe

Schipperke 'little boatman', 'little captain'

Schnauzer schnauze = 'snout' or 'muzzle'

Shih-tzu Chinese name for 'lion dog'

Terrier 'earth dog'

Whippet a word meaning 'to move briskly'

Xoloitzcuintle a name for the Mexican hairless dog, so called in honour of the god Xoloti.

Name Calling

Look in my face. My name is Used-to-Was.
Henry Duff Trail
After Dilettante Concetti

Me name is Mud.
Clarence James Dennis
The Sentimental Bloke

Iktis Names

In an article for *The Field*, Iktis said that a Scandinavian guest Gun inquired of him, 'How do you call your dog?' 'Like this,' he replied, producing a whistle, 'two peeps.' The question was repeated patiently until he realised that he was being asked for the dog's name, which was BOSS (she was a bitch). It was short for bossa nova; all the owner's dogs were named after Latin-American dances. Pondering on the subject of names, Iktis produced a list of some of the labels his friends had attached to their dogs. Apart from the unoriginal Bob:

ABERCROMBIE and BITCH (twin setters)

CHUCKLE, GIGGLE, TITTER and SNIGGER (quartet of terriers)

MR KERRY D (labrador retriever–D stood for Dog)

MISS MAM'SELLE SENORITA FRAULEIN MEMSAHIB (a poodle)

PUDDING (name given to his dog by an old music hall comic because it came after meat)

U-BITCH-U (duke's retriever)

U-TOO (pekingese)

The Hounds of Actaeon

ALCE (strength)
AMARYNTHOS (from Amarythia)
ASBOLOS (soot-coloured)

BANOS
BOREAS (north wind)
CANACHE (ringwood)
CHEDIAETROS
CISSETA
CORAN (crop-eared)
CYLLO (halt)
CYLLOPOTES (zigzag runner)
CYPRIOS (from Cyprus)
DRACO (dragon)
DROMAS (the courser)
DROMIOS (seize 'em!)
ECHNOBAS
EUDROMOS (good runner)
HARPALE (voracious)
HARPIEA (tear 'em!)
ICHNOBATE (track follower)
LABROS (furious)
LACAENA (lioness)
LACHNE (glossy coated)
LACON (Spartan)
LADON (from Ladon, Arcadia)
LAELAPS (hurricane)
LAMPOS (shining one)
LEUCOS (grey)
LYCISCA
LYNCEA
MACHIMOS (boxer)
MELAMPE (black)
MENELEA
MOLOSSOS (from Molossos)
NAPA (begotten by a wolf)
NEBROPHONOS (fawn-killer)
OCYDROMA (swift runner)
ORESITROPHOS (mountain-bred)
ORIBASOS (mountain ranger)
PACHYTOS (thick-skinned)
PAMPHAGOS (ravenous)
POEMENIS (leader)
PTERELAS (winged)
STRICTA (spot)
THERIDAMAS (beast tamer)
THERON (savage-faced)
THOOS (swift)
URANIS (heavenly one)

Rover by any other name

BAZZ was a collie cross named

after the cricketer Basil d'Oliviera

MORTIMER was a poodle named after Sir Mortimer Wheeler, the archaeologist, because he was always digging up old bones and had a fine moustache

OGGY was a Soggy Doggy who won first prize on a very wet day in a competition for the scruffiest dog

Names from a children's dog show in Sussex included:

BETA	POPPY
BONNIE	PRINCE
CHARLIE	SHEBA
FERN	TOPSY
FRIDAY	TRUCKA
HAPPY	TWITCH
HATTIE	WASTER
HOLLY	WEASEL
JANE	WILFRED
LASSIE	WINSTON
PEPSI	WISPA
PHOEBE	ZOLA

Traditional English dog names used for Battersea dogs in the Home's early days:

FIDO	SANDY
ROVER	SPOT
RUSTY	TOWSER

Body Bits

Ears (or Leathers)
Bat
Butterfly
Button
Rose
Tulip

Nose
Butterfly
Dudley
Smudge

Tails
Gawcie
Otter
Pipestopper

Rat
Ring
Sabre
Screw
Squirrel
Teapot

General Features
Applehead
Catfoot
Cheeky
Cobby
Cow-hocked
Dish-faced
Harefoot
Hucklebones
Pig jaw
Rockinghorse

Botanical Dogs

'Dog' used in descriptions of plants usually means common, inferior, or worthless as food for man.

Dogberry (wild cornel-tree or bloody-branched dogwood)

Dogbramble-Gooseberry (Canadian Ribes cynosbati)

Dogbrier (wild rose)

Dog-Daisy (common or ox-eye daisy)

Dog-Grass (eaten by dogs as an emetic)

Dog-Hip or Hep (fruit of the wild rose)

Dog-Leek

Dog-Lichen

Dogparsley (fool's parsley)

Dogrose (the common wild rose, Rosa canina: the Greeks used its roots to cure a bite from a mad dog)

Dogstones (vulgar name for the male Orchis)

Dogtooth Violet (Erythronium)

Dogtree (spindle, elder, guelder rose, dogwood)

Dogviolet (unscented wild violet, Viola canina)

Dogwheat (couch grass)

Dogwood (Cornus)

Dog's Bane (Apocynum, Asclepiadacae–poisonous to dogs)

Dog's Cabbage (Thelygonum cynocrambe)

Dog's Fennel (mayweed)

Dog's Mercury (very common hedgerow plant, Mercurialis perennis)

Dog's Poison (common fool's parsley, or Aethusa cynapium)

Dog's-Tail Grass (Cynouros–rough and crested)

Dog's-Tongue (hound's-tongue, or Cynoglossum, soft to touch)

Dog's-Tooth Grass (Cynodon, a sand-binding dune grass)

Horeshound

Cynanchum (genus of poisonous herbs and shrubs, twining)

Cynapium (an alkaloid from Aethusa Cynapium)

Cynara (artichoke, so called because the hard spines look like dog's teeth)

Cynarhodium (botanical term for certain fruits like rosehip)

Cynarocephalae (name sometimes used for artichoke and thistle-type plants)

Cynodontium (genus of Urn mosses)

Cynometra (tree found in China and East Indies)

Cynomorium (chokeweed)

Cynorrhiza and **Cynosciadum** (umbelliferous plants)

Swimming, Flying and Other Unlikely Dogs

Dog-Ape

Dog-Bee

Dog Cockle

Dog-Crab

Dogfish

Dog Louse/Tick

Dog-Salmon

Dog Whelk

Dog Winkle

Wagtail

Dog Destinations

Black Dog, Devon

Blackdog, Grampian

Canisbay, Highlands

Curbar, Derbyshire

Curbridge, Hampshire

Curbridge, Oxfordshire

Curland, Somerset

Dogdyke, Lincolnshire

Dogmersfield, Hampshire

Dog Village, Devon

Hound Green, Hampshire

Houndsditch, London

Houndslow, Borders

Houndwood, Borders

Hounslow, Middlesex

Huncoat, Lancashire

Huncote, Leicestershire

Hundalee, Borders

Hundleby, Lincolnshire

Hundon, Suffolk

Hunmanby, Yorkshire

Hundson, Hereford

Hunspow, Highlands

Hunstanton, Norfolk

Hunstanworth, Durham

Hunston, Suffolk

Hunston, West Sussex

Hunstrete, Avon

Hunton, Kent

Hunton, Yorkshire

Hunwich, Durham

Hunworth, Norfolk

Houndsditch (a place for burying dead dogs)

Isle of Dogs (so called because Edward III kept greyhounds there—or might be a corruption of 'Isle of Ducks').

Proverbial Dogs

A black dog has walked over him.

A cat and dog life.

A dog in a doublet. (A bold, resolute fellow.)

A dog in one's doublet. (A false friend.)

A dog in the manger.

A good dog deserves a good bone.

A living dog is better than a dead lion.

A well-bred dog hunts by nature. (Bon chien chasse de race.)

An old dog for a hard road.

Barking at the moon.

Barking dogs seldom bite.

GGRARF ARF ARF

Barking up the wrong tree.

Between dog and wolf. (The hour of dusk.)

Blush like a black dog. (Not to blush at all.)

Brag's a good dog but Holdfast is better. (Talking is all very well, but doing is better.)

Brag's a good dog if he be well set on but he dare not bite.

Call off the dogs. (Give up an enquiry.)

Crooked as a dog's hindleg.

Die like a dog. (Die in shame or misery.)

Dog bites dog. (Said of actors criticising each other.)

Dog eat dog.

Dogged as does it.

Dressed like a dog's dinner. (Dressed up flamboyantly.)

Enough to make a dog laugh.

Entre chien et loup. ('Owl-light' time—the best time to talk of difficult things.)

Every dog has his day. (Hodie mihi, cras tibi.)

Give a dog a bad name and hang him. (Slander succeeds!)

Give a dog a bone in his mouth and you may kick him and he can't bite.

Give him the dog to hold. (Play a mean trick on him.)

Go to the dogs.

He has not a dog to lick a dish. (He has nothing left.)

He who has a mind to beat his dog will easily find a stick. (Where there's a will, there's a way.)

He worries the dog. (Said of a visitor whom even the dog doesn't welcome.)

Help a lame dog over the stile.

His bark is worse than his bite.

Hungry dogs will eat dirty pudding.

'I am his Highness's dog at Kew; Pray tell me, Sir whose dog are you?' (Engraved on the collar of a dog given by Alexander Pope to Frederick Prince of Wales, and sometimes quoted at a pompous person.)

Is thy servant a dog, that he should do this thing!

It's a bad dog that deserves not even a crust.

It was the story of the dog and the shadow.

Lead the life of a dog.

Let sleeping dogs lie.

Like a dog in shoes. (Making a pattering sound.)

Like St Roch and his dog. (Inseparable.)

Little dogs start the hare but great ones catch it.

Love me, love my dog. (Qui aime Bertrand aime son chien.)

Not fit to turn a dog out in.

Not to have a word to throw to a dog.

Old dogs will not learn new tricks.

Put on the dog. (Behave in a conceited manner.)

Rain cats and dogs.

Sick as a dog.

The dogs have not dined. (Your shirt is hanging out at the back.)

The dogs of war. (The horrors of war, especially famine, sword and fire.)

The foremost dog catches the hare.

The hair of the dog that bit you.

The hindermost dog may catch the hare.

The more I see of men, the more I love dogs.

There are more ways of killing a dog than by hanging.

There's a black dog sitting on your back. (You're depressed.)

Throw it to the dogs.

Trust not a horse's heel nor a dog's tooth.

Walk the black dog in. (Punishment by fellow prisoners.)

What! Keep a dog and bark myself?

Whose dog is dead? What dog's a'hanging? (What's up?)

You can never scare a dog away from a greasy hide. (It is difficult to break a bad habit.)

You may know a gentleman by his horse, his hawk and his greyhound.

Dog Dictionary

Most of the words and phrases including 'dog' are derogatory—which is unfair to dogs!

Dog-and-Driver Chuck—in 1863 a drill piece described as a 'very common and exceedingly useful chuck' known also as the carrier chuck

Dog-Ape—baboon with dog-like head

Dog-Basket—old slang for a container for scraps for the dog

Dog Before Its Master—nautical term for a sea swell

Dog-Belt—broad waist-belt used by miners for hauling

Dogberry—an ignorant, self-satisfied, overbearing but good-natured night watchman in Shakespeare's *Much Ado About Nothing*—hence an officious and ignorant Jack-in-office

Dog-Biscuit—army mattress

Dogbolt—term of contempt

Dog-booby—awkward lout

Dog-buffer—dog stealer in the old days (he sold the skins and fed the carcase to other dogs)

Dogcart–cart for carrying sporting dogs (rather than a cart drawn by dogs), later a two-wheeled horse-drawn trap with seats back to back

Dog-Cheap–extremely cheap–cheap as dog's meat or offal

Dog Collar–clerical or woman's stiff collar

Dog Days–period when the Dog Star rises and sets with the sun (usually 3 July to 11 August), once thought to be a time when dogs were especially susceptible to rabies

Dogdraw–'a manifest deprehension of an offender against the venison in the forest, when he is found drawing after the deer by the scent of a hound'

Dog-Eared–(of a book) with pages turned down like a dog's ear, thus generally shabby

Dog-Eat-Dog–ruthless pursuit of self-interest

Dog-End–cigarette stub

Dog-Fall–in wrestling, when the two combatants touch the ground together

Dog-Fancier–receiver of stolen dogs which he would then 'find' for their owners, for a fee; later a breeder or seller of dogs

Dogfight–confused scrap

Dogged–sullen, sour, morose, surly, severe

Dogger–Dutch fishing-vessel used in the German Ocean in the 19th century, particularly for herring fishing, equipped with two masts (main and mizzen)

Dogger–in mining, a hard useless stone, generally a compound of silica and iron

Dogger–to cheat or sell rubbish

Doggerel–worthless verses

Doggerman–a sailor on a dogger

Doggers–a sort of stone found in English alum works with the true alum rock

Doggery–manifest cheating or nonsense; doggish way of doing things; dogs, collectively; rabble; drinking den

Doggess–polite way of calling a woman a bitch

Dogget–Dogget's coat and badge (from the actor Thomas Dogget, died 1721)

Doggish–churlish, growling, snappish, brutal

Doggo–hidden

Doggone–'dog on it', American expression of annoyance ('dog' is often used on oaths instead of 'God')

Doggy/Doggie–doglike; fond of dogs; dashing; in coal-mining, middleman's underground manager; cavalry officer's servant; type of collar

Dog-Head–hammer of a gunlock (the part which bites or holds the flint); kind of ape with doglike head; head of nail formed of rectangular projection

Dog-Hearted–cruel, pitiless, malicious

Doghole–a place fit only for dogs, a wretched dwelling

Dog-Hook–hook for leading a dog (1631); wrench for uncoupling bar rods; spanner; iron bar with bent end for grappling logs etc.

Dog-House/Hutch–dog kennel; place of disgrace

Dog in a Doublet–a bold, resolute fellow or a proud one (boar hounds in Germany and Flanders used to wear buttoned doublets when hunting)

Dog-in-the-Manger–one who will not let anyone else enjoy what he himself has no use for

Dog-Latin–'mongrel' Latin, for example the following definition of a kitchen:
'Camera necessaria pro usus cookare; cum saucepannis, stewpannis, scullero, dressero, coalholo stovis, smoak-jacko; pro roastandum, boilandum, fryandum et plum-pudding-mixandum'

Dog-Leach/Leech–a quack, a dog-doctor

Dog-Leg–bent like a dog's hindleg, e.g. staircase, fence, golf course fairway; chevron for an NCO

Dog-Letter–the letter R (because it sounds like a growl)

Dognail–nail with large and slightly countersunk head; large nail with head projecting on one side

Dog-Ribs–a tribe in North West Canada

Dog-Shooter–19th-century military volunteer; also RMA cadet not willing to be an engineer

Dogshores–pieces of timber used to shore up a vessel before it is launched

Dog-Sick–thoroughly sick

Dog Skin–leather made of real or imitation dog's skin

Dogsleep–light sleep, like a catnap, easily interrupted (dogs often seem to sleep with 'one eye open'); pretended sleep

Dogstone–a stone used for a millstone

Dog-Throw–lowest throw at dice

Dog-Tired–completely worn out

Dogtooth–pointed moulding like projecting teeth, used in later Norman architecture; also a sharp-pointed tooth growing between the front teeth and the grinders (eye-tooth)

Dogtooth-Spar–calcite crystals, looking like canine teeth

Dogtown–community of prairie dogs

Dogtrick–mean trick; brutal treatment

Dogtrot–gentle jog

Dogvane–nautical term for a small vane which shows wind direction and aids navigation, made of thread, cork and feathers and fastened to a half pike placed on the weather gunwale; also a cockade

Dog-Walloping–picking up cigarette ends

Dog-Watch–on board ship, a watch of two hours instead of four

Dog-Whipper–beadle who used to keep dogs away from churches

Dog-Whipping Day–18 October (St Luke's Day); it is said that a dog once swallowed the consecrated wafer in York Minster on that day

Dogsbody–originally nautical slang for pease pudding, or a dish of ship's biscuit with sugar and water, or a junior officer or

general drudge

Dog's Chance–only a bare chance

Dog's Dram–a spit into his mouth and a smack on his back

Dog's Home–guard-room

Dog's Lady–polite way of calling a woman a bitch (also DOGGESS, PUPPY'S MAMA, DOG'S WIFE etc.)

Dog's-Lug–bight in a sail's leech rope

Dog's Nose–man addicted to whisky; mixture of gin and beer

Dog's Portion–a lick and a smell, i.e. almost nothing; also refers to a man who admires women from a distance

Dog's Tooth–broken check pattern used in tweed-weaving

Coydog–cross between a coyote and a domestic dog

Hangdog–with a sneaky or cowardly look or manner.

The Thracian Dog was Zoilus, a carping Greek critic in the 4th century BC.

Like curs, our critics haunt the poet's feast,
And feed on scraps refused by every guest;
From the old Thracian dog they learned the way
To snarl in want, and grumble o'er their prey.

Pitt: *To Mr Spence*

less retractile than a cat's and are blunted almost as much as a dog's

Cyanthropy–a mania in which the patient thinks he is a dog and begins to bark etc.

Cynic–means a snarling, churlish person. Diogenes, pupil of Socrates, made famous an ancient school founded by another pupil (Antisthenes) and known as the CYNICS because the school was held in a gymnasium known as CYNOSARGES, or WHITE DOG (because a white dog once carried away part of a victim who was being offered there to Hercules). The effigy over Diogenes' pillar was a dog. The inscription was:

'Say, dog, I pray, what guard you in that tomb?'
'A dog.' 'His name?' 'Diogenes.' 'From far?'
'Sinope.' 'What! who made a tub his home?'
'The same; now dead, amongst the stars a star.'

Cynicspasm–a convulsion during which the patient howls like a dog

Cynegetics–the art of training and hunting with dogs

Cynography–a history of the dog

Cynolyssa–hydrophobia, or canine madness

Cynorexia–canine appetite; insatiable hunger.

'Kyon' Words

Kyon is the Greek root pertaining to dogs.

Cynailurus–the 'hunting leopards'; the name combines KYON for DOG with AILOUROS for CAT, because their claws are

'Canis' Words

Canis is the Latin root referring to dogs.

Canes Venatici–the Hounds or Greyhounds, a northern constellation, held in a 'string' by Bootes and surrounded by Bootes, Coma Berenices and Ursa Major

Canicular–belonging to the Dog Star; very hot time of year.

D.O.G.

The Dog of God–Laplander term for the bear, which has 'the strength of ten men and the wit of twelve'.

The word DOG, all by itself, has many meanings apart from the obvious one of Canis familiaris:

An iron hook or bar with a sharp fang at one end which could be easily driven into timber and thus used to drag something by means of a rope (nautical)

Andiron, or hook for holding logs

Cock of a gun

Gripping appliance

Heavy ostentation

Male of various animals (e.g. fox, ape, otter)

Spurious, base, inferior; very, utterly

To follow closely; to urge; to worry

To follow insidiously or indefatigably

To hunt or fasten with dogs

Dog was also a term used in the past for 'fellow', e.g.:

Gay Dog (always out and about and enjoying himself)

Dirty Dog (morally filthy, or one who talks and acts nastily–the French say 'Crotte comme un barbet', or 'Muddy as a poodle')

Sad Dog (much the same, but with a touch of reproof)

Surly Dog (with a surly temper)

To quote Boswell:

'I love the young dogs of this age; they have more wit, and humour, and knowledge of life, than we had.'

The same might be said of many four-legged dogs!

The whole charm of a dog lies in the depth of the friendship and the strength of the spiritual ties with which he has bound himself to man.

Konrad Lorenz
Man Meets Dog

*Go, like the Indian, in another life
Expect thy dog, thy bottle, and thy wife.*

Alexander Pope
An Essay On Man

THE END

Photographic Acknowledgements and Picture Sources

We wish to thank the following museums, institutions and individuals by whose kind permission the illustrations are produced, with special thanks to the many breeders who supplied us with photographs.

Cover design: David Roberts
Cover artwork: Robert Heesom
Cartoons on pages 24, 71, 108, 110, 111, 114, 120–4: Robert Heesom
Line drawings on pages 48, 56, 60, 61, 62, 65, 69, 70, 72, 74, 79, 81, 82, 83: Lorna Turpin
Title page: Ch. Cannobio Teddybear and Denverley Top of the Bill (Joan Danvers)

In the Beginning
6 Tate Gallery; 8, 9, 10 British Museum; 12 Ashmolean Museum.

Man, Woman & Dog
18 Copyright reserved. Reproduced by gracious permission of Her Majesty, The Queen; 20 Courtesy of National Film Archive/Stills Dept; 21 Tate Gallery; 22 Natural History Museum; 24 Courtesy of National Film Archive/Stills Dept; 30 Both pictures courtesy of Sotheby's; 31 Lesley Scott Ordish; 37 Guide Dogs for Blind Association; 38 Royal Air Force; 40, 41 Imperial War Museum; 42 Royal Air Force; 43 Imperial War Museum; 44 National Canine Defence League; 46 Photograph by permission of the British Union for the Abolition of Vivisection; 47 Scottish Tourist Board; 48 Mrs P. F. Luckhurst; 53 Tate Gallery; 54 Kennel Club.

Well-Bred Dogs
57 (above) Kath Hindley; 57 (below) Joan Danvers; 58 (above) Stuart Finley-Bisset; 60 Kentish Mercury South East; 61 Mrs H. E. Mitchell; 63 Max Jones; 64 Brenda Jones; 66 A. H. & S. A. Robinson; 67 Mr C. Woodhall; 69 Dr Brian Sproule; 73 Joan Danvers; 75 Yvonne Knapper; 76 Guide Dogs for Blind Association; 78 Kath Hindley; 79 'Monty, alias Montmorency of Hollesley' owned by Mr R. Simon of Wilmington, Sussex; 80 Mrs P. F. Luckhurst; 81 Trish Gilpin; 82 (below) Mrs R. Furness; 84 Ernest W. Albright; 86 (above) Max Jones; (below) Stuart Finley-Bissett.

Cultured Dogs
88 Both pictures courtesy of the Brontë Society; 89 Courtesy of National Film Archive/Stills Dept; 90 National Galleries of Scotland; 92 Courtesy of Vivian Noakes, author of Edward Lear 1812–1888, published by Weidenfeld & Nicolson 1985; 93 Wales Tourist Board; 94 National Gallery; 96, 97 Tate Gallery; 99 In the collection of the Duke of Buccleuch, KT, at Bowhill, Selkirk, Scotland; 101 Peter Spurrier, Portcullis President; 102–5 Courtesy of National Film Archive/Stills Dept; 108 (above) Courtesy of ICI Paints Division; (below) Courtesy of British Shoe Corporation Ltd; 112 From the Guinness Book of Pet Records by Gerald L. Wood.

In a Word
116 Courtesy of National Film Archive/Stills Dept; 117 National Galleries of Scotland; 127 'Rags' appears by kind permission of John O'Brien.